# Pills, Pesticides
# & Profits

# Pills, Pesticides & Profits

*The International Trade in Toxic Substances*

**Ruth Norris**
*Editor*

*Contributors*
**A. Karim Ahmed**
*Senior Staff Scientist*
*Natural Resources Defense Council*

**S. Jacob Scherr**
*Senior Staff Attorney*
*Natural Resources Defense Council*

**Robert Richter**
*Independent Film Producer*

**NORTH RIVER PRESS, INC.**
Croton-on-Hudson, New York

Library of Congress Cataloging in Publication Data
  Main entry under title:

  Pills, pesticides & profits.

    Includes index.

    1. Drug trade — United States. 2. Hazardous substances — United States. 3. Pesticides industry — United States. 4. Export marketing. 5. Underdeveloped areas — International business enterprises. I. Norris, Ruth, 1952-  II. Ahmed, A. Karim, 1939-  III. Scherr, S. Jacob, 1948-  IV. Richter, Robert, 1929-
    HD966.5.P54   382'.4566'00973   81-11001
    ISBN 0-88427-050-5   AACR2

For additional copies of this book, write to North River Press, Inc., Box 241 Croton-on-Hudson, NY 10520. For information concerning a student edition and other educational materials related to the book, write to the Council on International and Public Affairs, 777 United Nations Plaza, New York, NY 10017. For information on rental or purchase of the films whose transcripts appear in Appendix 1, write to Robert Richter Productions, 330 W. 42nd Street, New York, N.Y. 10036.

*Typography and Design by Diana Levine Computer Typesetting Pelham, New York*

Manufactured in the United States of America

# Contents

APPENDICES

*(A final section titled "Export of Toxic Substances — A Resource Guide" follows the Index only in the Student Edition of this book.)*

# Acknowledgments

The preparation of this book would not have been possible without the help of a number of individuals, many of whom spent endless hours gathering background materials and verifying factual information used in the book. The authors are particularly grateful to Katherine Gass, who carefully researched the materials for chapters III and V and helped in the preparation of the early drafts of these chapters; to Vincent Coluccio, for his extensive help in the preparation of Chapter II; and to Karen Holmes, who most ably helped gather trade and manufacturing data for chapter I and prepared drafts of Chapter IV Special thanks are also extended to Lauren Jacobson and Lisa Aronson, who assisted in redrafting certain sections of the book by painstakingly checking original source materials and clarifying obscurities in the text.

The authors also wish to acknowledge the assistance received from the following individuals, who provided useful comments on draft sections of the book: Ward Morehouse, of the Council on International and Public Affairs, New York; Barry Castleman of the School of Hygiene and Public Health, Johns Hopkins University; Dr. Robert Harris, a former member of the White House Council on Environmental Quality; and Dr. Rashid Shaikh, of the Harvard School of Public Health.

Finally, the authors wish to thank the Jessie Smith Noyes Foundation for its support of the research undergirding this book, and for helping to make possible a student edition and the Resource Guide bound into it.

# CHAPTER I
# THE INTERNATIONAL TRADE
# IN PESTICIDES AND
# PHARMACEUTICALS

The international trade in pesticides and pharmaceutical products, many of which are classified as toxic substances, looms for the 1980s as an international problem of potentially immense magnitude. Until recently, only the United States and other industrialized countries appeared concerned with health and environmental problems caused by unsafe pesticides and drugs. The bulk of these produces were, after all, manufactured, purchased, and used in developed countries. While global manufacturing patterns have remained essentially unchanged, dramatic increases in the trade of pesticides and drugs between developed and developing countries have occurred in the past decade. What was once a matter of national concern and debate has quickly become an issue of international importance.

International trade in chemical substances grew at an exponential rate in the 1970s. World trade in chemical products increased well over fourfold between 1970 and 1978, from $22 to $96 billion.[1] During the same time, the export of chemical products (which includes pesticides, drugs, and industrial chemicals) from developed countries to the Third World rose from $5 billion to $24 billion, an increase of close to 500 percent.[1]

Manufacturing corporations of almost all industrialized countries have engaged in some of the export practices known as "dumping": turning to Third World markets to sell or dispose of products banned or not approved by the government of the home country. Some recent examples from the United States are:

• In 1975 alone, the U.S.-based company, Velsicol, sold to some thirty countries more than three million pounds of leptophos ("Phosvel"), a pesticide which had never been approved by the federal Environmental Protection Agency for use in the United States. In Egypt, leptophos, which causes damage to the nervous system, killed more than a thousand water buffaloes and poisoned dozens of farmers.[2]

• In April 1977, the U.S. Consumer Product Safety Commission banned the sale of infants' sleepwear treated with the flame retardant TRIS, which was discovered to be a carcinogen. Before the U.S. government put a halt to the practice, 2.4 million TRIS-treated garments were exported, primarily to Third World countries.[3]

• In 1977, the U.S. Food and Drug Administration removed the drug dipyrone from the market because it had been shown to cause a severe blood disorder which interfered with white blood cell formation, and because it had been implicated in several deaths. Yet as of January 1982, U.S. companies continued to sell dipyrone in Latin American countries for use against minor ailments, without warnings concerning its dangerous side effects.[4]

• In 1979, Nedlog Technology Group, based in the United States, offered a $25 million payment to the president of Sierra Leone for rights to export hazardous wastes from the United States for disposal in Sierra Leone. Only after adverse publicity revealed the nature of the illicit deal did the president withdraw his consideration of the project.[5]

Similar cases of dumping continue to increase at a rapid pace. This practice can be linked in part to the adoption of stringent regulations on pesticides, drugs, consumer products, and hazardous wastes by agencies of the United States and other industrialized countries, especially during the past ten years, making it easier and more attractive financially to operate in relatively unregulated Third World markets. With much lower levels of consumer awareness and few independent sources of information about the adverse effects of these products, Third World markets look especially inviting.

## Historical Perspective

In 1828, the German chemist Fredrich Wöhler made an unexpected and startling discovery. While carrying out in his laboratory a routine experiment with an inorganic substance, ammonium cyanate, he was able to synthesize for the first time an organic compound, urea — an excretory product of many animal species.[6] Wöhler's accidental discovery proved to be a major turning point in the history of science and industrial technology. Although little noted and only grudgingly accepted in its day, the event has had a far-reaching impact to this day. The synthesis of urea, produced artificially and without the aid of living cells, had ushered in a new era of industrial development — the introduction of tens of thousands of man-made chemical substances into commercial use, first in the highly industrialized countries of the northern hemisphere, and more recently, throughout the world.

Until the early nineteenth century, the nature of the so-called organic compounds, substances derived from living sources, was a matter of some dispute. The great French scientist, Antoine Lavoisier, had discredited the prevailing theories of chemical combinations and reactions which were based on the notion that chemical substances contained an incorporeal, fiery fluid which escaped during combustion.[7] But many leading biologists and chemists continued to believe that organic substances were produced in living systems through a "vital force" which could not be duplicatd in the laboratory from mineral or inanimate ("inorganic") sources. In the context of such beliefs, the explosive nature of Wöhler's discovery becomes clear. The initial experiment and subsequent laboratory synthesis of other organic compounds, radically changed the scientific community's fundamental understanding of chemical substances.

Thus, by the middle of the nineteenth century, a new generation of European scientists, abandoning the prejudices of their predecessors, was busily engaged in synthesizing scores of organic substances in the laboratory. Synthetic organic chemicals began to be produced on an industrial scale and applied in new commercial products. With the establishment of the synthetic dye industry toward the end of the century, first in Germany and later in Britain, the burgeoning chemical industry came of age, producing not only primary industrial chemicals, such as soda ash, sodium bicarbonate, and sulfuric acid, but also a myriad of complex organic compounds, such as aniline dyes and substituted aromatic hydrocarbons, which were principally derived from coal-tar sources.

During the early part of this century, the chemical industry grew and matured in Europe and in the United States; by the 1920s it had become an important factor in the economic growth of most industrialized countries. The use of industrial chemicals had widened greatly by the beginning of World War I. In addition to the dye and armaments industries, manufacturing and processing of chemicals became important to the agricultural, pharmaceutical, and other industries. The introduction of new drugs, food additives, cosmetic ingredients, synthetic fertilizers, and insecticides — all of which depended on the expanded production of a vast spectrum of chemical substances — rose at a steady rate through the first four decades of the twentieth century. For example, in the United States, the chemical industry production increased about sevenfold from 1900 to 1939.[8]

However, the greatest increases in chemical production came during and after World War II. In the United States, research and development on a number of new synthetic products, such as rubber and other polymers, was initiated because of wartime shortages caused by the loss of some of the main sources of natural products. These technological ventures stretched the resourcefulness of the chemical industry to its full potential. Almost overnight, whole new industries were built, and they have continued to flourish to this day. Since World War II, chemical industry production has risen dramatically in the United States and the rest of the world. Figure 1 shows the increase for the United States. According to the U.S. chemical industry production index, annual manufacture of chemicals increased more than 900 percent between 1947 and 1978.[8,9]

**Figure 1. U.S. Chemical Production Increase
Between 1900 and 1978**

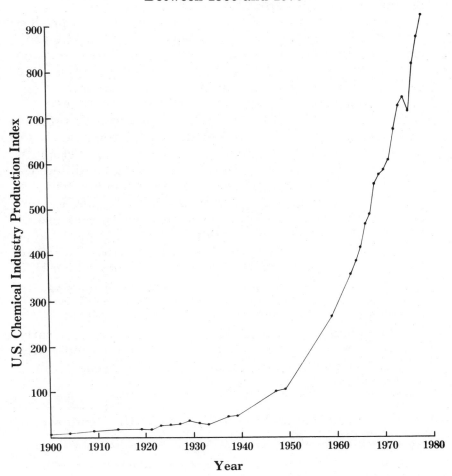

Important changes were also occurring within the chemical industry. Petroleum and natural gas had replaced coal as the primary feedstock materials for synthesis of many organic chemicals. This conversion, in turn, led to the development of the present petrochemical industry. The manufacture of synthetic polymers, produced from petrochemical derivatives, became a growth industry of extraordinary proportions. Polymers are used in a variety of manufactured products, such as synthetic fibers, plastics, coating materials, and pliable elastomers. They make possible such products as vinyl floor tiles, plastic milk bottles, and an almost limitless number of consumer products.

In the early 1970s, the average annual increase in production of the U.S. chemical, industry was a healthy 6.4 percent, but in the latter half of the decade, this figure rose to an even more impressive 9.4 percent. In contrast, during the same periods, average annual production increases for all manufacturing industries in the United States were 4.0 percent (70-74) and 6.6 percent (75-79).[8,9] Similarly, annual growth rates in the chemical industries of other developed countries were greater than growth rates in other manufacturing sectors. In Japan, West Germany and France, this margin of difference was often between two and three percentage points.[8,9]

Consumption patterns in the industrialized countries further illustrate the rapid growth in production and use of chemicals. Estimated consumptions of chemicals per head of population in the United States rose from $160 in 1963 to $290 in 1973, to $495 in 1977, the last year for which U.S. data was available. Comparable consumption figures for West Germany are $130 in 1963, $306 in 1973, $487 in 1977, and as high as $745 in 1979.[8,9] Similar consumption increases were found in France and Britain. These statistics clearly point to an industry that is vigorous, expanding and above all, has the ability to continue selling its products in a worldwide market.

## Growth of the Pesticide and Pharmaceutical Industries

As World War II ended, agricultural use of insecticides, herbicides, and commercial fertilizers began to increase rapidly. Most of the recently introduced pesticides and fertilizers are manufactured from petrochemical feedstock materials, and their production costs are extremely sensitive to changes in the price of crude oil.

During the 1960s and 1970s, large-scale Western agricultural technologies were introduced to many traditional farming societies in Third World countries. This was spurred by the so-called "green revolution," which boosted crop yields by introducing such capital-intensive and chemical-dependent practices as mechanical farming and use of commerical fertilizers. The "green revolution" also brought dependence on a variety of synthetic pesticides and herbicides. In many tropical countries, pesticides such as DDT, dieldrin, and endosulfan have also been used extensively for malaria control and as a preventive measure against other insect-borne diseases. Both programs contributed to unprecedented increases in the importation of pesticides by developing countries. From 1974 to 1978, Third World imports of pesticides increased from $641 million to almost $1 billion.[10] Thirty-eight percent of the international trade in pesticides in 1978 occurred in developing countries.[10] Pesticide consumption in African countries increased fivefold from 1964 to 1974, while import of pesticides in the Philippines grew fivefold in the six-year period, 1972-1978.[11]

Trade statistics for the United States show the growing importance to pesticide manufacturers of pesticide exports. In a period of just two years, 1976 to 1978, U.S. companies increased their pesticide exports from $625 million to $1 billion.[12] Although U.S. production of pesticides rose by half during the 1970s, exports to foreign countries increased by 200 percent.[12] According to a report by the U.S. Congress' General Accounting Office, 30 percent of all pesticides exported from the United States were unregistered—that is, not approved by the federal Environmental Protection Agency—for use in the United States. Approximately 20 percent of these unregistered pesticides were formerly registered but suspended or canceled for most uses after dangers became apparent.[13]

The chief exporters of pesticides are companies based in Germany (25 percent of the market), the United States (20 percent), the United Kingdom (15), Switzerland (15), France (13), Japan (5), and Italy (3). Taken together, these seven countries account for nearly all of the pesticides imported by developing countries. Only 4 percent of the international trade in pesticides originated in the Third World in 1978.[14]

The practices of these companies, and the consequences for residents of developing nations, are explored in detail in Chapter Two.

\* \* \*

Drugs and other chemically therapeutic substances have been used in treating human disease since the beginning of recorded history. Nearly every traditional system of medicine, some of whose practices continue in developing countries, depends on the use of medicinal plants, minerals, and other natural extracts. The twentieth century brought a virtual revolution in chemotherapy, with almost universal reliance on drugs and chemical agents in the treatment of diseases. The introduction of sulfa drugs in the 1930s, closely followed by the discovery of penicillin and the extensive use of antibiotics after World War II, led to the establishment of the modern pharmaceutical industry. Today, sale of drugs makes the pharmaceutical industry one of the most profitable of any manufacturing industry. Moreover, most drug sales are made by a small number of major multinational corporations. The fifty largest firms account for two-thirds of drug sales, and 90 percent of world production is supplied by the top 110 firms.[15]

As is the case with other chemical substances, most drugs are produced in the developed countries. Of the $30 billion drug production in non-socialist countries in 1973, about 90 percent occurred in developed countries. The largest producer of drugs was the United States (34 percent), followed by Japan (20 percent) and West Germany (13 percent).[15,19] International trade in pharmaceuticals between 1965 and 1976 rose from $1.2 billion to $4.5 billion.[15] In Third World countries, drug sales during the 70s increased at an annual rate of

20 percent; most of the drugs were imported from Europe and the United States. West Germany is the leader in international drug trade (Western European countries account for nearly 75 percent of exported drugs). The United States, with 20 percent of the international trade, ranks second.[16] The United States and Britain in 1973 exported the largest quantities of pharmaceuticals to Latin American countries, with 35 percent and 20 percent of the market, respectively. West Germany was the major exporter to Western Asian countries with 22 percent of the market, followed by Britain (21 percent) and Switzerland (18 percent). However, for the rest of the Asian market, the United States was once again the major exporter (27 percent), with West Germany a close second (25 percent).[15] Another indication of the growing U.S. share of the world market is the rising export trade of U.S. drug companies. In 1979, foreign sales volume of U.S.-based firms increased at nearly twice the rate of domestic sales.

International trade has become increasingly important to pharmaceutical companies as the patents of their best-selling drugs expire, and as the process of introducing new drugs to the developed world requires longer periods of testing and certification. It has been estimated that of the 200 top selling brand-name drugs in the United States, 104 patents had expired by 1980.[15] Stringent safety and efficacy requirements established in recent years by the U.S. Food and Drug Administration (FDA) for all new drugs means that companies can introduce fewer new drugs than they have in the past. In 1980, for example, of the total 2,452 new drug products introduced on the world market, only 104 were launched in the United States and Canada. In contrast, more than 1,000 new drug products were introduced in Third World countries.[17] The United States Food, Drug and Cosmetic Act also prohibits the export of any drug not approved by the FDA, though there appears to be no provision to ban the export of drugs whose approval has been subsequently lifted by the agency.[18] These inhibitions on drug manufacturers – increased research and development costs, long lead time before approval is given, and the export prohibition – have led U.S. firms in recent years to move their chemical testing facilities abroad. This has resulted in the introduction of only

marginally tested new drugs in foreign markets, before the
manufacturer could comply with FDA requirements in the
United States.

In the past several years, some developing countries have
encouraged the manufacture and importation of "generic,"
name drugs, those without patent protection. These drugs'
prices are significantly lower than those of patented products, allowing consumers considerable savings. This is
especially important in developing countries, where it has
been estimated that drug expenditure constitutes 40 to 60
percent of individual medical care costs, compared to 15 to 20
percent in the industrialized countries.[15] Thus, any lowering
of drug costs bears significantly on the quality of health care
available to the less affluent populations. At present, 15,000
brand-name drugs are sold in India, and 14,000 in Brazil. In
the United States and some European countries, tens of
thousands of brand-name drugs are also available.[20] However, there is no indication that such a proliferation of drugs
is necessary to maintain good health. For example, in Norway
and Sweden, there are only 2,500 and 2,000 brand-name
drugs, respectively, available on the market.[21] There is no
evidence that lack of additional drugs has had any adverse
health impact on Scandinavian people. In the past decade,
because of the pressure placed on multinational corporations
to lower drug costs, many firms have introduced "branded-
generic" products to the international market. These products are so named because they can still be sold under their
brand names but at a reduced price. The expiration of patents
on these drugs opened the market to increased competition,
thereby lowering prices. In the future, "branded-generic" products may dominate the international trade in pharmaceuticals, particularly in the Third World markets.


* * *


Exports to the developing world of pesticides, pharmaceutical products, processed foods, medical devices, infant
formulas, and other consumer products are not, in and of

themselves, the problem. Abuses, exploitation of uninformed consumers, and the double standard that says products considered unsafe for use in the industrialized world may be promoted and sold freely in the developing nations—these are the issues confronting the governments and citizens of the United States and Europe. Drugs dispensed without prescription, sold improperly labelled, and without adequate warnings, appear to be the rule, rather than the exception, in many Asian, African, and Latin American countries. Ineffective and obsolete products, which cannot be sold in Western markets, are regularly "dumped" on Third World countries. The indiscriminate promotion of infant formula milk products to impoverished and ill-informed consumers in developing countries continues, in spite of efforts of international organizations and authorities to address the issue. Sales of banned or highly restricted drugs and pesticides continue to plague the Third World despite the best efforts of national and international bodies to publicize the dimensions of the problem.

In this book, we make a preliminary presentation of the best known cases that have been brought to our attention. We believe that we are now witnessing only the early signs of a growing problem—one in which increasing production of chemicals in the more highly developed countries will inevitably lead to the search for markets in the less developed parts of the world. This trend can only accelerate as domestic consumption in developed countries reaches a saturation point and as new laws restricting the use of hazardous products are enacted and strictly implemented. Production of industrial chemicals used in manufactured products continues to rise in almost all industrialized countries.

The international trade in pesticides and pharmaceuticals poses a set of immensely complex technological and economic issues which form the basis of much international debate. Increases in worldwide production of chemicals alone would lead to greater export of manufactured products from developed to developing countries, particularly in the consumer goods industry. Multinational firms are expanding their markets in the Third World and they appear to thrive in a climate of "benign" neglect by the governments of developing countries. Agencies and authorities in the industrialized countries continue to tolerate a "double standard" when it comes to regulating the flow of hazardous and highly restricted products in the international market. "Banned at home but okay abroad" seems to be the operating principle. We have attempted to present a broad and, we hope, representative picture of this growing problem in international relations. It is an issue that individuals, as well as governments, in industrialized and developing countries can ill afford to ignore.

# CHAPTER II
# PESTICIDES

Achedemade Bator is an isolated village on the shore of Lake Volta in Ghana, West Africa. Its population is almost entirely illiterate. The people are fishermen who get their protein and their income, as well as their drinking water, from the lake.

When imported pesticides became available in Ghana, the fishermen of Achedemade Bator, like those of other villages, discovered what seemed to be a remarkably effective, easy, and profitable way to increase their catch. They bought the insecticide Gammalin 20, which Ghana's Ministry of Agriculture had provided for cocoa farmers, poured the chemical into the lake, waited for fish to float to the surface, and then gathered them — salting, smoking, or selling whatever was not needed for their immediate consumption.

Gammalin 20 is a trade name for lindane, which is produced in the United States by Hooker Chemicals & Plastics Corporation, in West Germany by Celamerck Gmgh and Company, in France by Rhone-Poulenc, and in Great Britain by a subsidiary of ICI Limited.[1] It is highly poisonous. People who are exposed to lindane may experience dizziness, headaches, vomiting, diarrhea, convulsions,[2] brain disturbance, muscle spasms, or unconsciousness[3]. Long-term exposure can cause liver damage,[2] and some researchers believe that lindane may play a role in the develoment of such serious blood disorders as aplastic anemia and leukemia.[3]

But the farmers and fishermen of Achedemade Bator knew little or nothing about the effects upon their health of the

13

poison they were pouring into Lake Volta. To them, lindane was simply the easiest, cheapest method for catching fish. Some villagers experienced symptoms of lindane poisoning, but did not connect the symptoms with eating fish from Lake Volta. Many of those who knew of the poisoning believed that the poison stays in a fish's head, and that cutting off the head made the flesh safe to eat, although housewives could identify a contaminated fish from a non-poisoned one by its smell.

The fishermen knew something was wrong when the fish population of Lake Volta began to decline at a rate of 10 to 20 percent per year. But they blamed the scarcity on natural causes and kept up their catches by using more and more lindane. This killed many other plants and animals in the lake in addition to fish.

A Ghanian organization called Association of People for Practical Life Education turned the situation around. The group taught the villagers of Achedemade Bator about the connections between fishing with poison, symptoms of lindane poisoning, and the lack of fish in Lake Volta. The village witch doctor, very influential in village affairs, agreed that poisoning fish was bad, and during a ritual ceremony, he issued a taboo on the use of Gammalin 20. Other village leaders obeyed the taboo, and as a result, the villagers of Achedemade Bator have returned to using nets and traps instead of poison to catch fish. [42]

Consciousness raising and education make the story of Achedemede Bator one of success. But in villages throughout Ghana, fishing with poison continues. In Ghana and in the developing nations of the world, fishing is just one example of the widespread misuse of dangerous chemical pesticides. Lindane. Aldrin. Dieldrin. DDT. Dozens of synthetic pesticides that are banned or severely restricted in the industrial nations where they are produced remain in use in the Third World. In what is apparently  a case of corporate "dumping" of products avoided by informed consumers, pesticides — both safe and unsafe — are freely exported from industrial nations to the Third World, where their use is heavily promoted by pesticide sellers, and by government policies as well.

The dangers are staggering. Every year, the World Health Organization estimates, five thousand people die and half a million more are poisoned by direct contact with pesticides. More than half the fatalities are children.[26] [27] Pesticide products are freely sold to buyers in less-developed countries where there are no facilites for regulating hazardous chemicals — indeed, where few people understand that chemicals are dangerous and that precautions must be taken in order to avoid exposure. Some developing countries have virtually no laws controlling pesticide imports, registration, and handling, and few maintain any facilities for monitoring pesticide residues in food or in the environment.[5]

In addition to harming human health, the unregulated use of hazardous pesticides throughout the world is creating ecological damage, contributing to the development of chemical-resistant strains of pests, and contaminating food and fiber products imported by the United States and other developed countries where the pesticides originated. Despite these problems, however, the production and exportation of these pesticides is actually increasing. A travelogue of consequences:

• Leptophos, a pesticide produced in Texas by Velsicol Chemical Corporation, was exported between 1971 and 1976 to developing countries, including Colombia, Egypt, and Indonesia. In Egypt, leptophos was blamed for the deaths of several farmers. Whole rural families became afflicted with convulsions, speech difficulties, lack of bladder control, and other problems. More than a thousand water buffalo became paralyzed and died.[6] Even after these poisonings occured, even after the pesticide's potential to harm neurological systems was discovered in laboratories in the United States, aggressive corporate touting of the safety of leptophos continued.[5]

In 1976, however, workers at Velsicol's Texas plants began to show symptoms of severe neurological damage, partial paralysis, impaired vision, and dizziness. Their medical records indicated the employees had symptoms suggestive of demyelination or encephalitis. Diagnosing physicians found four workers to have multiple sclerosis, two to have psychiatric disorders, three to have encephalitis, encephalomyelitis, and post-infectious encephalomyeloradiculitis, respectively.[3] Only after this domestic tragedy was production of lepthophos in the United States finally stopped.[5]

• The World Health Organization's 1976 report on occupational health states, "In some countries field surveys of poisoning among spraymen exposed to agricultural chemicals revealed an average prevalence of up to 40 percent of workers with symptoms of poisoning during a spraying period.[5] Instructions about safety and proper uses are passed haphazardly from dealers to farmers by word of mouth. Those who actually apply pesticides by hand or by backpack sprayer in the fields have little notion of the dangers of the product they are handling.[5]

• In Guatemala, according to *The New York Times,* the western hemisphere's highest yield of cotton (as of 1977) was matched by the world's highest level of pesticide spraying. Farmers had switched from DDT, to which pests had largely become immune, to organophosphate pesticides. Those organophosphate-based pesticides have an advantage (from a public health viewpoint) over DDT and its relatives, the chlorinated hydrocarbon pesticides, in being less persistent in the environment. But organophosphate-based pesticides are much more acutely poisonous to humans and therefore require extreme precautions in use.[3,4,18]

Villagers in La Noria, Guatemala, reported that sometimes they were not even warned when spraying was about to take place and had to run for shelter when planes sprayed pesticides on cotton fields. A nurse at a clinic near La Noria reported treating thirty to forty patients per day for pesticide poisoning: "The farmers often tell the peasants to give another reason for their sickness, but you can smell the pesticides in their clothes."[7] Guatemalan government figures show 1,039 cases of pesticide poisoning in 1976, none of them fatal. But doctors, priests, and village leaders said there were many deaths from pesticide poisoning, and a much greater number of nonfatal poisonings.[7]

The workers who bore the brunt of these risks were Indians, migrant workers from the highlands who earned $1.25 for a twelve-hour shift, and who might work the fields for one to three months at a time. "The Indians are ignorant of the dangers of pesticide poisoning. They eat sweet-tasting cotton buds that have been sprayed, they enter the fields too soon for washing and drinking from the polluted irrigation canals.[7] Many die and many more become ill,"[8] reported *The Times.*

Studies on the health effects of such exposures are difficult to conduct, particularly where the victims are migrant workers. Villagers living near the cotton fields, however, were studied by the American Research Industry and found to have levels of DDT in their blood nearly seven times higher than their counterparts in urban areas.[7] DDT contamination of cow's milk is about 90 times that permissible in the United States, where the use of DDT is prohibited.[15] The level of DDT in the blood of the people themselves in Nicaragua and Guatemala is 31 times greater than that in residents of the United States.[15] In Nicaragua as in Guatemala, local sources say that the number of deaths due to pesticide poisoning is probably much higher than the 383 recorded by government analysts during 1969 and 1970.

• In 1969, in the Mexican state of Tijuana, seventeen people died and three hundred became ill after they consumed sugar that had been contaminated with parathion[2], an insecticide which is restricted in the developed world because it is highly toxic. A teaspoonful can kill an adult man.[39] It is readily taken into the body by inhalation or absorption through the skin,[1] and has caused the most fatal poisonings of any organophosphate pesticide.[3] Parathion is manufactured by Bayer AG in West Germany, Cheminova in Denmark, and Monsanto Agricultural Products in the United States.[1]

• Malathion, used for control of malaria-carrying mosquitoes in Pakistan, in 1976 poisoned some 2,500 workers, of whom five died. Malathion is not considered exceptionally dangerous, but studies of the incident showed the pesticide had contained impurities which made it especially toxic. "This incident is believed to have been partly caused by failure to use elementary precautions during the handling and spraying of the formulation," said a report. "[I]t thus shows that despite clear handling and packaging labels poor handling practices will occur . . . in developing countries."[10]

• In Peru, pesticide spraying on cotton eradicated all bird life in the area around the cotton fields and resulted in government action to control the use of dangerous pesticides.[11] But while government controls apply to large-scale applications, farmers in remote areas can still obtain, without appropriate technical assistance, several pesticides banned or severely restricted in the countries in which they are produced.[11]

• In Thailand, as of 1979, more than one hundred kinds of dangerous chemicals were being mixed to produce more than a thousand brands of pesticides, mostly for use against pests that destroy portions of Thailand's rice, maize, bean, vegetable, sugarcane, tapioca, rubber, and fruit crops. "Thai farmers or even agricultural scientists are much more interested in using pesticides to protect their production than giving heed to the devastating effects of pesticides," complains Dr. Prayoon Deemar of the Ministry of Agriculture and Cooperatives. The pesticides, he says, only keep a loss that remains at the same level every year from expanding further. Dr. Prayoon surveyed five major markets in Bangkok and found pesticide residues in more than 40 percent of the vegetables for sale and three-quarters of the samples of rice and flour in his sample. Every kind of freshwater fish was contaminated, as were nine of twenty milk supplies and 58 of 69 cooking oil samples.[12] In a single province of Thailand in the four years ending in 1970 twenty-four people are reported to have died, and 320 more suffered illness due to pesticide poisoning, in a population of 3,789.[13]

• Trinidad and Tobago's Ministry of Health reported 293 known deaths from pesticide poisoning in 1977. The government of Trinidad and Tobago enacted legislation for the first time in 1980 to begin to study and control the import and sale of pesticides.[13]

• In Nairobi, Kenya, Robert Richter, was able to buy, over the counter, a number of hazardous pesticides that are restricted in the United States because their use poses unreasonable risks to human health and the environment. These included aldrin and dieldrin, the most acutely toxic of the organochlorine (DDT-related) pesticides, and known animal carcinogens;[3] benzene hexachloride (BHC), banned in the United States after tests showed it caused tumors and reproductive problems in mice, even when absorbed in tiny concentrations;[15,16] paraquat, a herbicide that became known in connection with its application to marijauana fields in Mexico, which has a history of accidents and has been known to poison humans; and chlorfenvinphos, acutely toxic when absorbed through the skin.[17]

Considering the high illiteracy rates and often repressive working conditions in developing countries, it is not surprising that pesticide handlers and farm workers in those countries are poisoned by pesticides. Workers are often unaware of what chemical they are using, how it should properly be used, and the hazards with which it is associated. They are ignorant of the hazards to which they expose themselves and others. It has been argued that the dangers to which farm workers and the public in these countries are exposed are a regrettable by-product of the extraordinary effort necessary to produce enough food for hungry populations. However, in many developing nations, the majority of pesticide use occurs on cash and export crops that cannot be consumed by the people who bear the greatest risks from the use of these chemicals.[15] In Latin American countries like Guatemala or Honduras where cotton is a major crop, 50% of all pesticides used may go only to cotton. If bananas are also a major crop, pesticides applied to these two crops alone may be at least 85% of the country's total pesticide consumption.[40] The hazards of excessive pesticide use affect the developed world as well as the nations of the Third World, by damaging the global environment, by creating resistant strains of pests that in turn carry new outbreaks of diseases once considered under control, and by contaminating products that find their way to all parts of the world, including those countries in which the pesticides originated.

## Threats to the Global Survival System: Environmental Damage, Super Pests

In the late 1940s, DDT was introduced as the major tool in the worldwide program to eliminate malaria, by killing the disease-carrying mosquitoes that caused it to spread. The initial result was a dramatic reduction in the incidence of

malaria — and a worldwide proliferation of synthetic, or man-
made, pesticides. The belief that these chemicals provided a
panacea for all pest problems was widely held.

That belief was false, and dangerous, for two reasons. DDT
and its chemical cousins proved to be a threat to human
health and to the survival of birds and fish. And the pests
that were supposed to be eliminated quickly evolved resistant populations against which the pesticides were ineffective except in larger and larger doses. Today, malaria and
other insect-borne diseases are making a worldwide come-
back.

DDT, dichlorodiphenyltrichloroethane, with its breakdown
products TDE and DDE, has become the most thoroughly
studied of the chemically related group of pesticides known
as chlorinated hydrocarbons. The group includes aldrin,
dieldrin, benzene hexachloride (BHC), lindane, chlordane,
heptachlor, DDVP, endrin, Mirex, toxaphene, and methoxy-
chor, among others.

DDT seemed relatively innocuous at first. Like many other
chlorinated hydrocarbon (also called organochlorine)
pesticides, it is not acutely — that is, immediately and fatally
— toxic to humans, although in fairly large doses it can
disrupt the nervous system, heart, liver, and respiratory
system.[18] DDT is also not readily absorbed through the skin,
so exposure from handling the pesticide has not resulted in
many serious poisonings.[3] But over time, DDT proved
dangerous enough. Used on a variety of food and nonfood
crops, as well as in the worldwide malaria control program,
DDT was implicated in the declining populations of seabirds
such as the herring gull, brown pelican, and double-crested
cormorant, and birds of prey, such as the bald and golden
eagles, and the California condor, now nearly extinct. DDT
poisoning caused the birds to form thin-shelled eggs that
broke before healthy chicks could hatch.[14] DDT was also
blamed for fish kills[14], and laboratory tests convinced scientists that long-term exposure to DDT may have cancer-
producing effects.[2,3].

One of the chief dangers of DDT and its organochlorine
relatives proved to be their ubiquitousness. These chemical
compounds are extremely stable, persisting in the environ-

ment for many years. (The half-life of DDT, or time it takes for half a given mass to degrade, is twenty years.) They dissolve readily in fat rather than in water and therefore build up in the fatty tissues of animals, concentrating to increasingly harmful levels as they make their way up the food chain from fish to birds, from grazing animals to other predators, including humans. DDT cannot be confined to the area in which it is used. Its high vapor pressure facilitates the evaporation and movement of DDT throughout the atmosphere. DDT has infiltrated practically everything – the air we breathe, the water we drink, and the food we eat.[2] DDT has been discovered in migrating birds, fish, and seals in Antarctica, thousands of miles from the nearest point of use, and in the deepest parts of the oceans.[2]

In the United States, all crop uses of DDT were banned in 1972, and all uses except in certain emergency conditions were banned in 1973[3] on the grounds that continued use would pose an unacceptable risk to humans and to the environment. But a ban in one country does little to protect people or the environment from a pesticide as persistent and difficult to contain as DDT if the chemical remains in use elsewhere. By now it should come as little surprise that it does. DDT continues to be produced in the United States by Montrose Chemical Corporation, which informed the EPA that it had sold the pesticide to twenty-one overseas importers in the one-and-one-half-year period ending in November 1980.[41]

DDT is also produced in France, Italy, Spain, India, Mexico and Argentina. An example of the way in which the chemical is distributed and promoted in Third World countries comes from an international fair in Nairobi, Kenya, where hundreds of farm chemicals were on display. A sales representative was interviewed by Robert Richter:

Q: What is this composed of?

A: That I don't know.

Q: Is it a safe product?

A: It is a safe product. The common name we use here is Kombi. Pesticide for cotton. It is made of DDT, and it is safe to use.

Although DDT has been publicly withdrawn from the market in Kenya, its sale and use continue. It is widely applied to cotton and maize, and it is available in such commercial brands as Safi-Safi, Didimac, Didifog, and Kensd D5.[19]

Tragically, the ever-increasing risks to which we all, but especially farm workers, are exposed count for steadily diminishing returns in terms of pest control. The pests are winning.

Many insects have short generation times, and some produce more than one generation per year. When a pesticide application kills all but the resistant individuals in an insect population, the survivors quickly produce a new generation which inherits their resistance to the pesticide. Successive generations exposed to pesticides show increasingly greater proportions of resistant individuals. This effect was demonstrated in a laboratory experiment with a common fruit fly species (Drosophilia melanogaster). After fifteen generations of the fly were exposed to DDT, the amount of DDT required to kill significant numbers of the flies had increased by thirty times.[20]

The effect is as well documented by field experience as in laboratories. The increase in the number of the world's pest species resistant to chemical pesticides has accelerated sharply since 1947 with the development and widespread use of synthetic pesticides.[21] A survey by the Food and Agriculture Organization Panel of Experts on Resistance to Pesticides has documented the increase in the number of resistant strains of insects and mites.[21] In 1965 the panel found 182 resistant strains, and by 1977 the number of resistant strains had reached 364.[21] Surveys also confirmed the connection between repeated exposure to the same pesticide and development of resistance among pests. For example, the reported increase in resistance of mosquitoes to dieldrin between 1955 and 1960 was concurrent with the use of dieldrin in the World Health Organization's campaign to eradicate malaria.[21]

The first approach to the problem of pesticide-resistant strains of insects was the development and application of new synthetic chemical pesticides.[21,22] Typically, several types of pesticides would be used in succession, with a chemical being replaced whenever it had lost its effectiveness against the target species.[22] But then a new trouble developed, in the form of insect pests that became resistant to not just one but many pesticides. Double, triple, and quadruple-resistant pests, immune to a broad range of pesticides, began to be discovered, greatly increasing both the growth and the magnitude of the resistance problem.

The development of these "super pests," resistant to chemicals commonly used to control them, has had devastating economic effects in countries all over the world. For eight years, cotton growers in Texas and northern Mexico had successfully used methyl parathion against the tobacco budworm, but in the late 1960s this cotton pest became resistant even to high concentrations of the pesticide, and that particular control mechanism ceased to be economically feasible. Crop damage was so great that the cotton industry, which had been the economic mainstay of northern Mexico, collapsed. The economic and social stability of the small towns in the region was upset as many farm workers moved in search of work.[9] By 1979, Colombia had lost half of its cotton crop due to increased insect resistance to pesticides. Although Colombia has usually been an exporter of cotton, projections by the Cotton Growers Federation indicated that the nation would have to import 30,000 tons in 1980.[23] Similarly, in the Canete Valley of Peru, the DDT and chlorinated hydrocarbons that were used to eradicate the cotton pests also killed birds and other animals. Pests that became resistant to DDT and the other chemicals flourished without the natural predation that had once kept their populations in check.[24]

Where pests thrive, of course, the problems that they create multiply, and the damage affects human health as well as economics. Sri Lanka once had as few as twenty-three cases of malaria in a whole year, but is now experiencing two million cases a year, or about the same as before malaria control was applied. Overuse of agricultural pesticides is believed to have been a cause.[13] In India, where cotton growers used three million kilograms of DDT in 1970 to produce just over five million bales of fiber, DDT use had doubled but cotton yields remained the same six years later. The noticeable difference that resulted from increased use of DDT was a corresponding increase in the incidence of malaria in cotton-growing regions. Over the same six years, the number of people afflicted with malaria in India rose from 60,000 to five million.[25] The story is repeated in Central America. The incidence of malaria in El Salvador had decreased from 70,000 to 25,000 cases a year, but by 1976, following the increase in the use of DDT, it had risen again to over 80,000 cases. Honduras and Costa Rica have also experienced a dramatic increase in the incidence of malaria, but these two countries are not major cotton producers. In this case the misuse of pesticides was responsible for epidemics not just in the producing nations but in neighboring countries as well.[25]

The development of multiple resistant species of mosquitoes has, in fact, dimmed the hopes for total eradication of malaria. The World Health Organization has documented an increase in multiple resistance among the world's populations of anopheles mosquitoes that carry malaria. As many as 43 species of mosquitoes were resistant to one or more pesticides by 1976.[21]

Nor is multiple resistance the only danger of using different pesticides in succession to control increasingly resistant pest populations. Pests can also acquire cross-resistance, using the same metabolic defenses that protect them from one group of pesticides to acquire resistance to pesticides to which they have not even been exposed. One of the reasons given for the doubling in malaria cases in El Salvador (33,000 cases in 1973 to 66,000 in 1974) was resistance to the insecticide carbamate acquired by mosquitoes that had been exposed to another organophosphate pesticide, parathion, used for agricultural purposes.[5]

Pest resistance developed through overuse of pesticides, including the resurgence of malaria due to pesticide overuse in more than a dozen countries, is recognized as a serious worldwide problem. According to the United Nations Environment Programme's 1979 *Report on the State of the World Environment,* the resistance problem could have a grave impact on the economy and effectiveness of global pest management programs, with resulting adverse effects on global food production and public health.[21]

UNEP's preference for a worldwide pest management program is a system of careful monitoring of pest species, carried out by government extension services, whose personnel advise health and agriculture workers on pest control methods — which may include such non-chemical approaches as biological control (for example, releasing sterilized male insects to inhibit reproduction among fertile females), environmental control (release of natural enemies to control pests), and genetic alteration (to inhibit a species' success in maintaining a healthy population).[21] These procedures are beginning to receive widespread acceptance in the United States and other developed nations. Unfortunately, this integrated pest management technique requires that all parties involved — government officials, agriculture and health workers, private distributors of pest control products, and farmers — have a fairly extensive understanding of ecosystems, the role of pests and predators, and the importance of coordinating efforts. In many developing nations that expertise is simply not available, and the philosophy that "more is better" when it comes to pesticide use continues to prevail, with disastrous results.

"When DDT was first used on cotton," observes Robert Richter, "it was applied only once or twice a year. But the insects did not all die . . . newer and more resistant insects developed, requiring newer and more powerful poisons to kill them. Now cotton is sprayed in some Latin American countries an average of twenty-eight times a growing season."[42]

## The Boomerang Effect

Even if pesticide contamination of the environment could be contained within the boundaries of those Third World countries where hazardous pesticides are sold and used, the chemicals would still pose a threat to people in other nations as well. For what is exported is, in turn, imported. Some of the foods on which those pesticides are used — beans and peppers from Mexico, coffee and beef from Central America — come right back to the consumers of the United States and the rest of the industrialized world. For example, a 1978 FDA study of coffee imported to the United States showed that 45 percent (25 out of 55) of the samples had illegal residues of pesticides. All of these pesticides, including DDT, benzene hexachloride (BHC), lindane, dieldrin and heptachlor, were ones whose use within the United States had been prohibited or severely limited.[30] This is called the "boomerang effect." And the contamination of coffee may be only the proverbial tip of the iceberg.

In the United States, where agricultural imports in 1977 totaled more than $13 billion, it is the job of the federal Food and Drug Administration to assure consumers that food reaching the marketplaces is safe, pure, and wholesome. But according to a 1979 General Accounting Office report to Congress, the FDA "has identified neither the pesticide practices of, nor all pesticides used in, other countries. Such knowledge is essential if the agency is to make sure that food imports do not contain harmful residues of pesticides that have been suspended, canceled, or never registered in the United States."[27]

Indeed, test methods used by the Food and Drug Administration cannot detect residues of many pesticides used outside the United States. The FDA does not sample all significant food commodity imports for pesticide residues. When contaminants are found, the agency does not consistently try to identify the contaminant, its origin, or its potential danger to human health.[27]

The FDA estimates that approximately one-tenth of the food imported into the United States contains illegal residues of pesticides.[15] That figure may be low. In its 1979 report, the General Accounting office revealed that FDA analytical methods *could not detect* 178 pesticides for which tolerances — allowable residue levels — have been established. Nor can FDA testers assure consumers that imported food is free of some 130 commonly used pesticides for which tolerances have not yet been set.

The true extent of pesticide residues returning by way of imported food is simply not known. Nor is it known what effects these residues may have on the health of consumers. Nevertheless, there are grounds for concern. When DDT and dieldrin were used in the United States, studies showed that both chemicals (part of the organochlorine pesticide group) had accumulated in human tissues at levels comparable to the levels found in laboratory animals that had developed cancer as a result of their exposure to the pesticides.[28] Although there is no absolute proof that DDT and dieldrin cause cancer in humans, they have, as previously noted, been banned for all but a few emergency uses in the United States since the early 1970s. Still, the American consumer is not necessarily safe. DDT residues above permissible levels were detected in half a million pounds of beef imported from El Salvador in 1976. (Having detected the residues, the USDA rejected that quantity of beef at the international boundary.[27] But questions remain as to whether contaminated beef may sometimes escape detection.) In fact, the General Accounting Office estimates that 14 percent of the meat consumed in the United States, a significant proportion of it imported, is contaminated with illegal residues of pesticides.[15]

Is the boomerang effect a sort of macabre justice to the countries that allow the continued production and exportation of hazardous pesticides? Perhaps, if the "boomerang" could be counted on to return to the country from which it was "thrown." But it's not truly a boomerang. Hazardous pesticides may return to the country where they were produced, or they may find their way into other importing countries, or even be consumed, in the form of residues on food, right in the country to which they were exported.

A case in point is a crop of tomatoes, bound for United States purchasers from Mexico in 1980. The tomatoes turned out to be contaminated with celathion, one of a group of pesticides that are generally quite poisonous in small doses. Celathion is manufactured by a German-based corporation, Celamerck. Use of celathion on food crops is prohibited both in the United States and in Mexico, but Mexican farmers, who are permitted to use the chemical for controlling pests on cotton, had used it illegally on tomatoes and cucumbers as well. In this case the "boomerang" was more like a hot potato. Tossed out by a German manufacturer, appearing and rejected at the United States port of entry, the celathion apparently made its way to the systems of Mexican consumers who bought rejected tomatoes that had been sold at a cut rate to local markets, once again in defiance of local law.[31] So the same Third World countries that are the markets for banned and restricted pesticides may also become the market of last resort for whatever contaminated foods the inspectors of the developed nations discover and reject.


## Whose fault?

DBCP is short for dibromochloropropane, a soil fumigant that was produced and formulated at eighty United States plants since the mid-1950s. As early as 1958, the chemical had been linked with reproductive disorders in experimental animals, and that information was made available to at least two of the main producers of DBCP (Shell Chemical Company and Dow Chemical Company) within a few years. Nevertheless, it was not until 1977, after as many as three thousand workers who had been exposed to DBCP became sterile or nearly sterile, that the United States Government banned most domestic uses of the product. It is still used in Hawaii, where it is injected into the ground on pineapple farms.[38]

The U.S. ban did not halt DBCP production. As recently as early 1980, DBCP was produced for export by Amvac Chemical Corporation.[15] And in May 1981, the president of an Arizona firm, Gowan Chemical Company, pleaded no contest to charges of selling and distributing DBCP in the United States. He was sentenced to six months in jail, a $2,000 fine, and three years' probation.[29]

The story of DBCP illustrates several points. Most important, perhaps, is that workers, and the general public as well, cannot be assured that the chemicals to which they are exposed in their work and in everyday life are safe unless the producers of those chemicals are monitored and regulated by outside agencies with power to enforce whatever restrictions are necessary to protect health and safety. In the United States, although there has been a long process of trial and error, during the course of which many people have been found to be suffering health effects from exposure to chemicals once regarded as safe, a fairly elaborate system of regulations and controls has evolved. But the situation changes at the international boundary.

No pesticide may be sold in the United States unless it has been registered by the federal Environmental Protection Agency (EPA). Registration is granted only after the agency is satisfied that the product's social and economic benefits outweigh its risks, and that the product, when used according to commonly recognized practice, can safely and effectively perform its intended function without posing unreasonable risks to human health and the environment.[29] If evidence becomes available after a pesticide has been registered that indicates the product does pose unreasonable risks to health and environment, a procedure known as RPAR (Rebuttable Presumption Against Registration and Continued Registration) may be instituted. Unless, as the procedure's name implies, the company holding registration can rebut charges against the product's safety, EPA may cancel registration, suspend registration while investigation is under way, or restrict the product to certain specified uses. Some pesticides allowed for widespread use may be used only by persons who are competent in the safe use of pesticides and knowledgeable about pesticide hazards, injury prevention, and recognition and handling of accidents.The EPA, as of 1981, had restricted forty-one products to use by certified applicators.

Regulations covering who may purchase pesticides for what uses, however, do not apply to products shipped outside the United States. A pesticide produced solely for export need not be registered with EPA. Prior to 1978, it was possible to begin the manufacture and widespread distribution of a pesticide outside the United States without even informing the EPA, and over 85 million pounds of such unapproved pesticides were shipped abroad in 1975. In addition, pesticides which had been banned or severely restricted by EPA could be exported without any warnings to foreign purchasers or importing governments. In 1978, Congress moved to establish some controls on pesticide exports under the Federal Insecticide, Fungicide, and Rodenticide Act (FIFRA). Before shipping a banned or unapproved pesticide overseas, exporters must receive a statement from the foreign purchaser acknowledging his understanding that the pesticide cannot be sold or used in the United States. A copy of this acknowledgement statement is then submitted to EPA, which in turn sends it to the appropriate official in the importing country.

The 1978 FIFRA amendments also established new labeling requirements for exported pesticides. Labels for pesticides, registered or unregistered, shipped overseas must now meet most of the standards applied to pesticides sold in the U.S., including:

(1) False or misleading representations on the label are prohibited.

(2) The pesticide must not be an imitation of another pesticide.

(3) The label of the pesticide must bear the registration number of the establishment in which it was produced.

(4) The statements on the pesticide's label required under FIFRA must be conspicuous and in terms likely to be read and understood by an ordinary individual.

(5) The label must contain necessary warning or caution statements.

(6) If the pesticide is not registered in the United States, the label must contain a conspicuous statement to that effect.

(7) The label must contain an ingredients statement.

(8) The label must contain a statement of use classification ("general use" or "restricted use") under which the pesticide is registered.

(9) The container must bear a label providing the name and address of the producer, the name, brand, or trademark under which the pesticide is sold, the net weight or measure of the contents of the container, and the registration number assigned to the pesticide.

(10) If the pesticide is highly toxic, the label must bear the skull and crossbones, and the word "poison" in red, and information regarding an antidote.

The new export notification and labeling procedures for pesticides only entered into effect in Summer 1980. Some have argued that these requirements do not go nearly far enough and have called for strict licensing or total prohibitions of the sales abroad of pesticides considered too dangerous or too little studied for use in the United States. Nonetheless, the American pesticide industry has become very nervous about the existing procedures which at least increases the likelihood that foreign officials are being made aware of the regulatory status of pesticides bought from the United States. In June 1981, the National Agricultural Chemicals Association proposed amendments to FIFRA which would cut off communications between EPA and foreign governments concerning exports of banned pesticides and limit export notices to products which have never been approved by EPA for use in the U.S.

Even assuming that exported pesticides are shipped to Third World countries in properly labelled containers, to purchasers who have been informed of the products' risks, with the knowledge and consent of the purchasers' governments, we cannot conclude that workers in those countries, and residents of the areas where the pesticides will be used, have any protection. Informed consent on the part of the purchaser means little if the purchaser is simply a foreign subsidiary of the producing company. Government knowledge of purchases of banned pesticides is of little value if there is no regulatory capability in the importing country to stop the continued importation or prevent the improper use of those chemicals. All of these problems pertain, to some extent, to Third World countries.

Labeling requirements, for example, apply only to the container in which a pesticide is shipped. But corporations and farmers in many Third World countries now formulate pesticides — mix the active ingredient, or "technical ingredient," with inert ingredients, emulsifiers, baits, and so on — after the products have reached their destination. Local formulation is a rapidly increasing practice in the developing nations.[33] In many instances, formulators import ingredients in large containers clearly labeled with safety precautions and instructions for use, but then package individual allotments (work which is, incidentally, often performed by workers who do not have even elementary protective gear)[5] in unmarked containers. Results, once the pesticide reaches the market, can be disastrous. A visitor to Pakistan in 1974 reported seeing a customer purchase a pesticide: "[O]ne customer, lacking a suitable container, unwrapped his turban, poured a granular pesticide therein, and replaced it on his head for transport."[5] In a small town in Malaysia, consumer activist Cha Ket reported finding the herbicide 2,4,5-T, whose chief danger is in its frequent contamination with dioxin, one of the deadliest substances known, being sold in unlabeled bottles that were kept next to similar bottles containing sauce for cooking and eating.

Even where labels are used, they are meaningless to people who cannot read. Illiteracy rates are quite high in many Third World nations, particularly among villagers and farm workers who are most likely to come into direct contact with pesticides. If the pesticide user can read, a label is still meaningless if it is not written in the langauge of the reader. Pesticide labels are typically written in English.[42]

Assuming, however, that a Third World user of a pesticide product can read and understand the label, and proceeds to comply with instructions — two very large assumptions, as we have seen — there is still the potential that someone may be poisoned because the product has been inadequately labeled or deliberately mislabeled. In 1979 the Colombian government imposed financial penalties on Hoescht and Shell for selling mislabelled pesticides, also fining Hoescht, Ciba-Geigy, American Cyanamid, Velsicol and Dow Chemical Company for marketing defective or adulterated products. Over half of the pesticides for sale in Mexico are insufficiently or incorrectly labelled.[15]

So while there is some regulation of the traffic in hazardous chemical pesticides, it would be naive to assume that what regulations exist are sufficient to prevent the kind of pesticide exposure that goes on in the Third World every day. For a closer look at regulations — and loopholes — in action, there is the example of Colombia, a Latin American country where farmers, according to 1978 estimates by the national Agriculture and Livestock Institute, uses 17 million kilograms or 140 million dollars worth, of pesticides in a year.[23] Among the 638 pesticide products found to be available in that country are several that are banned or severely restricted in the developed world:

• DDT.
• Aldrin and its chemical relative, dieldrin, the most acutely toxic of the organochlorine pesticides. A teaspoonful to a tablespoonful, ingested or absorbed through the skin, can kill an adult man. These chemicals were once used heavily on cotton and other crops in the United States, until registrations for most uses were canceled in 1974 because of laboratory tests proved aldrin and dieldrin to be cancer-causing.[14]
• 2,4,5-T, the herbicide used for weed control on rangelands, airports, lumberyards, vacant lots; it is restricted because of its association with dioxin, one of the deadliest substances known. 2,4,5-T is a component of Agent Orange, the defoliant used in Vietnam which was later implicated as the cause of birth defects and infant deaths.[3][32]
• Mirex, used in the southeastern United States to poison fire ants until 1978, when it was banned because of concern over its potential to cause cancer, reproductive disorders, and environmental damage.[3][34]
• 2,4-D, although widely used in the United States, is restricted to nonfood crops and kept away from drinking water. It is a suspected carcinogen. Its use has been halted in the national park system of the United States because of concern and pressure on the part of environmental groups who raised questions about the chemical's potential to cause miscarriages and birth defects.[35]

Colombian people do suffer health effects from the widespread use of these pesticides, which researchers have found to be used indiscriminately, and with virtually no regulation.[42] A rash of miscarriages and deformed babies in the early 1970s has been linked tentatively to the use of 2, 4, 5-T.[38] In November 1976, six hundred persons, more than half of them children, were poisoned — after a bottle containing parathion broke while being transported and contaminated sacks of flour also carried on the same truck. The victims were poisoned when they ate bread baked from that flour. About a quarter experienced only mild symptoms, but a few showed symptoms of severe poisoning.[2] In El Espinal, a rice growing region where 96 percent of the people work with pesticides, farmers suffer a variety of illnesses traceable to

heavy crop spraying of pesticides. Physicians noted a significant increase since 1973 in the number of young men reporting sexual impotency problems concurrent with the local introduction of aerial pesticide application.[23] As the spraying
continued, physicians treating victims of pesticide poisoning
had to administer almost triple the normal dosage of an-
tidotes inorder to achieve a cure.[23]

These, however, are only a few incidents that have come to
light that point to the dangers of pesticide exposure. In most
of Colombia, as in most of the Third World, data on health effects is hard to come by. Information often must be obtained
from the workers themselves, and they are reluctant to com-
plain about work-related health problems because they may
lose their jobs if they do so. In some cases, workers may not
connect symptoms — headaches, nausea, muscle spasms,
rashes, vomiting, and so forth — with their exposure to
pesticides. Even if they do make the connection between exposure and symptoms and decide to report the problem, they
may not find authorities and health officials willing to listen.

"It's been five years that I've been working here in this
hospital," said a doctor in a hospital in rural Colombia. "And
during that time I've seen many cases of workers that have
come here with pesticide poisoning. Many of the patients
have been able to leave the hospital in fairly good condition,
but there are others who have died. It is certainly true that
the problem is of a much greater proporition than is usually
reported. Pesticide poisoning is the number one health problem that this hospital deals with. It seems there are certain
interests that want to keep the true proportions of this very
grave problem hidden."[42]

Government interests? Investigations in Colombia, as
elsewhere, have found evidence of official ignorance.

"We don't have the infrastructure in the country to deal
with the problem" said a spokesman for the Colombian
Ministry of Health. He acknowledged that his country has
"plenty of problems" handling a "very great increase" in
pesticide importation. It is the job of his Ministry to inform
the Ministry of Agriculture about possible health dangers
related to pesticide use. But when questioned about Mirex,
the fire ant poison suspected of causing cancer and environ-

mental damage, which is readily available to Colombian farmers, the Colombian Ministry of Agriculture official in charge of pesticides admitted that he had never heard of Mirex, didn't know its registration was cancelled in the United States or that it was sold in Colombia, and had not even heard that the U.S. Environmental Protection Agency publishes and distributes a list of banned products that may pose dangers to the health of citizens in countries where they are imported.

Colombia is far from unique in its official unawareness. This excerpt is from an interview with the director of a government farm in Bangladesh:

**Q:** Are there any products you are aware of that are prohibited in the West, the United States — pesticides and insecticides that are used here?

**A:** No, we get no such report, that you should not use such and such medicine, such and such pesticide. we don't get any report from anywhere, even from the producers also.

**Q:** So if a product was banned in the West, would you know about it here?

**A:** No, we don't know any banned items, whether these are banned by any other producing country, we don't know.[42]

That official ignorance shows up in documents related to the effects as well as the distribution of hazardous products. "Officially in Central America they refer to five thousand cases of pesticide poisoning," says Roberto Chediack, a pediatrician who has talked to hundreds of workers in a study of pesticide poisoning, "but we believe that this is really lower than the actual amount. There have been official meetings that agreed with us on this. In particular, in Costa Rica they say there are 1,500 cases in five years. We looked at a couple of hospitals, and found that in three months alone there were seven hundred cass of poisoning just in those three months. So in five years there would have been a lot more than they said."[42]

Unfortunately, ignorance invites itself to be taken advantage of. And finally, whatever can be said about government and other organizations failing to protect the workers and consumers of the world — and in the absence of a worldwide authority with the ability to enforce curbs on the growing traffic in hazardous pesticides – responsibility lies with the producers and sellers of dangerous agricultural chemicals. These companies, most of them multinationals, manufacture about four billion pounds of pesticides annually, or over a pound for each man, woman and child in the world, and export about a fifth of that.[15] Their overseas sales methods range from the unwise to the irresponsible.

"What we have is the transnationals who are promoting products in a way that is totally irresponsible," charges Jose Lutzenberger, an environmental leader in Brazil. "They have conditioned our farmers to use most of the products even unnecessarily. They have spread the philosophy of preventive use. So you use your poison on a certain day, not because you have a certain pest. Most of the time the farmer doesn't even know what a pest is. He confuses many of his natural predators, of his useful insects, with pests. They have been conditioned to use an insecticide anytime they see an insect flying around."[42]

Samuel Gitonga, chief agriculturalist of the Nairobi Irrigation Board, echoes that concern.

"Pesticide manufacturers normally have local representatives . . . inform potential buyers of their products. They come loaded with a lot of information – often information that one cannot read immediately – regarding the efficacy of the product and where it has been registered. It is very difficult for less developed countries, particularly small ones such as Kenya, to spare enough manpower to check and cross check all this information and to assure that the product has been registered in a given country as claimed . . . Possibly the less developed countries serve as a final testing ground before these products are released in the more developed countries."[39]

Testing ground or dumping ground, the Third World is in peril from those chemical pesticides. and as we have seen, it is a peril that cannot be ignored, or treated as an internal problem of the countries where pesticide use is allowed, because ultimately it is the danger, as well as the responsibility, of the rest of the world as well.

# CHAPTER III
# PHARMACEUTICALS

Drugs, like pesticides, can relieve ills or cause them. The difference is in the way they are prescribed and used, whether by knowledgeable, trained practitioners or haphazardly, by dealers whose motivation is to sell products and consumers who have no way of knowing whether any given product will be appropriate, effective, and safe. And the same double standard that applies to pesticides holds true in the case of pharmaceutical products. Formulations banned or restricted in the industrialized nations where they are manufactured are freely exported to the Third World, often unaccompanied by the research information that led to restrictions. Products that consumers in the United States and Europe would take only under a physician's supervision, and then only if prescribed in the treatment of a life-threatening illness, are sold over the counter, without restriction, in importing countries. People are being poisoned, and some of them are dying. Epidemics of typhoid fever proved nearly unstoppable in Mexico because the drug most effective against typhoid had been so widely sold and used that typhoid bacteria had developed a resistance. Health problems caused by poor nutrition and hygiene are inappropriately treated with drugs, rather than with education, improved diet, and sanitation. Tropical disease research lags while the sales of pharmaceuticals developed for use against the special health problems of the industrial world continue to increase, both in volume and in profits. And woe betide the unwary traveler taken in ill a Third World country.

## Prescription for disaster

Twenty years ago, Japan experienced a virtual epidemic of a nerve disorder called subacute myelo-optic neuropathy (SMON). The victims numbered in the thousands. Although no one is sure just how many Japanese suffered from SMON, two different surveys, by investigators for the Japanese government[63] and an independent epidemiological researcher[52] turned up at least 8,000, and up to 11,000 cases. SMON symptoms range from abdominal pain and constipation to loss of feeling, paralysis, blindness, degeneration of nerves and muscles, and death.[52] By 1978, at least seven hundred Japanese had died of SMON[63].

What caused the epidemic? Scientists suspected clioquinol, an amoeba-killing drug used in the treatment of amoebic dysentery. The drug, introduced in 1934 by the Swiss firm Ciba-Geigy, had shown side effects, including nerve disorders, in human and animal users shortly after it was first marketed,[63] and Ciba-Geigy's own experiments in 1939 and 1962 had shown that dogs given the clioquinol products Entero-Vioform and Mexaform often developed epileptic-type seizures and died.[11,63] But Ciba-Geigy and other firms continued to promote clioquinol as a remedy for all types of diarrhea, under a variety of trade names in Japan, including Entero-Vioform and Mexase, until 1970 when the firm withdrew two hundred products containing clioquinol from the Japanese market. Fewer than forty cases of SMON were reported in Japan the following year[52], strong evidence that the drug was the cause of the SMON epidemic.

The manufacturers of clioquinol, however, argued that the drug was not at fault. Industry representatives claim that the Japanese SMON epidemic was primarily a case of misuse of clioquinol-containing products by the Japanese. They exceeded the recommended dosages of the drugs, according to the drug firms, thereby exposing themselves to a greater risk of developing SMON*. Evidence indicates a greater risk of developing SMON when clioquinol is taken at high dosages.

---

*Other hypotheses put forth by drug companies, and immediately eliminated, proposed that mercury or other heavy-metal poisoning, agricultural chemicals, pesticides, or vitamin B-12 deficiencies could also have been responsible for the outbreak of SMON.[52]

In 1978, seven years or so after clioquinol products were withdrawn from the Japanese market, a Japanese court ruled that clioquinol was indeed to blame. "None of the proofs given in this case have substantiated that the disease is due to a virus or any other substance other than clioquinol," the court said. [17,63] Further, Ciba-Geigy officials had done "all they could to promote their [clioquinol products'] mass sale and consumption."[63] Ciba-Geigy and two Japanese companies, Takeda Chemical Industries and Tanabe Seiyaku, were held responsible for the SMON epidemic, along with a government agency, the Japanese Pharmacy Affairs Bureau. The court blamed the pharmaceutical companies for failing to warn physicians and consumers of clioquinol's dangers and for stressing false claims that the product was safe. By April 1980, Ciba-Geigy had paid settlements to more than 1,500 victims and survivors of victims.[63]

Japan's clioquinol disaster provided a clear warning. Clioquinol is no longer sold in the United States, Norway, Sweden, Denmark, or Great Britain. Australian and Venezuelan regulatory agencies allow clioquinol to be used only in severe cases of amoebic dysentery.[17] Conferees at the 1979 Kyoto International Conference Against Drug-Induced Sufferings published a statement in *The British Medical Journal* urging "those manufacturers who are still selling these products either to provide clear evidence that there are benefits which justify the risk or withdraw them."[38]

Ciba-Geigy and other manufacturers continue to advertise and otherwise promote clioquinol-containing products — Entero-Vioform, Mexaform, Marol, Mexase, Entox, Intestopan, and others — as treatment for a wide variety of intestinal disorders[8,9,49] in countries without the medical expertise or regulatory capability to evaluate the benefits and risks of clioquinol and then restrict its use. *The Drug Index for Malaysia and Singapore,* a prescribing guide for physicians, containing information supplied primarily by drug manfuacturers, lists Mexaform for "all forms of gastro-intestinal disorders."[17] Robert Richter was able to buy clioquinol-containing products over the counter in Asia, Africa, and Latin America.[49]

Thousands of miles from Malaysia, in Kenya, a *London Times* reporter read in a package insert in 1978, that Mexase,

another Ciba-Geigy clioquinol product, would cure "a feeling
of repletion, digestive insufficiency due to poor mastication,
or dietary errors."[9] And in Nigeria, Winifred Amene, a health
care practitioner who worked in a military hospital and then
at the University of Nigeria Teaching Hospital, wrote, "I cannot remember any doctor that did not prescribe Entero-
Vioform, especially if it was available in the pharmacy . . . The
drug was so commonly in use that all of [the doctors] must have
used [it] at one time or the other."[34]

The tragedy in this widespread use of a dangerous drug
against even minor illnesses is that much safer remedies are
available. Diarrheas are quite common in the Third World, caused, in many cases, by poor diet, contaminated water, or un-
satisfactory control of sewage. At the People's Health Center
in Bangladesh, paramedics teach villagers to treat their
children's diarrhea with a safe and effective home remedy —
a mixture of molasses, salt and boiled water.[49] This mixture
restores the body's essential electrolytes, allowing the child to
retain water and preventing the acute dehydration that can
cause death. Molasses provides a source of energy, helping to
keep the child strong enough to ward off the pneumonia that
often follows diarrheal disease in the Third World countries.

The tragedy is compounded as the availability and promotion of inappropriate or unsafe pharmaceutical remedies diverts
attention and money from preventative care, such as safer
water supply systems, sewage systems, and so forth. These
public and private health measures could prevent disease from
threatening in the first place.

In African nations, in Malaysia, and in Brazil, anabolic
steroids (synthetic derivatives of testosterone, the male sex hormone) have been sold over the counter, without prescription,
as an appetite stimulant, to promote weight gain and relieve
exhaustion, fatigue, and malnutrition, especially in children[8,48,49]. Boys and girls given these drugs can experience serious
and unpleasant side effects — in boys, sexual abnormality and
bladder irritation; in girls, extreme and usually irreversible
masculinization, including excessive hairiness, male pattern
baldness, deepening of the voice, and clitoral enlargement, as
well as later menstrual problems.[58,59,60] Pregnant women should
never take anabolic steroids because the drug can cause sex-

ual abnormality in fetuses.[15,60] In developing nations, neither product labels, package inserts, nor prescribing guides distributed to physicians tell the truth about these products: that they have *not* been proved effective, that they cause side effects, that their use in the developed world is severely restricted. In the United States, anabolic steroid products such as Winstrol, Anadrol-50, Adroyd, Anavar, Durabotin, Dianabol, and Maxibolin are used only as a supplement to other drugs and therapy and even then only for specific conditions — as in treating patients who have been burned or severely injured, elderly patients suffering from osteoporosis, a degenerative bone disease; and patients with certain types of anemia in which red blood cell production needs to be stimulated.[60] "Winstrol," warns *The Physician's Desk Reference,* the standard prescribing guide used by doctors in the United States, "should be used only after diagnois [of aplastic anemia] has been established." Third World consumers of Winstrol and other anabolic steroids, however, can buy them the way nineteenth-century Americans, prior to the passage of drug regulations, could buy remedies at county fairs and chautauquas. Parents can be taken in by the exaggerated claims for drugs like anabolic steroids — claims which drug companies are not permitted to make in developed countries. Nutritious food, not anabolic steroids, will promote weight gain and relieve fatigue in malnourished children. Like those nineteenth-century snake oils, anabolic steroids are likely to do more harm than good in masking the true cause of the child's poor health.

Some inappropriately used drugs make it more difficult for doctors to determine exactly what is wrong with the patient. Other drugs can actually compound illness, and even threaten the patient's life. That possibility arises with a vengeance in the case of the analgesic (pain-relieving) compounds aminopyrine and its derivative, dipyrone, manufactured by Hoechst of West Germany and a number of other multinational corporations. The two compounds are "about as effective [as] aspirin."[20] But aminopyrine and dipyrone are much more dangerous than aspirin. Although there is some controversy about the exact rate, of every thousand patients who take these drugs, as many as five or six develop a disease known as agranulocytosis, a form of anemia that robs the body of its infection-fighting white blood cells and makes the patient extremely susceptible to life-threatening infections.[8] In the United States, neither aminopyrine nor dipyrone has been available over the counter — that is, without a prescription — since 1938. Until 1977, when the U.S. Food and Drug Administration decided that the risks incurred by taking aminopyrine or dipyrone outweighed any possible benefits and banned the drugs,[36] the two compounds had been allowed only for treating terminally ill patients who did not respond to treatment with safer drugs[8] and for patients whose lives were threatened by extremely high fevers.[36] Australian and Swedish authorities have also banned aminopyrine and dipyrone, while its use is severely restricted in Japan and the Philippines.[17] Once again, the situation is different in Latin America, Africa, and Asia. A citizen of a developing country, consulting his local pharmacist about remedies for arthritis, a headache, lumbago, or a slight fever might well be sold aminopyrine or dipyrone. He would not, in most cases, have to have a physician's prescription, nor would he be likely to know of the risk he was taking. How many of these purchases have caused or will cause agranulocytosis? In most developing countries it is impossible to guess, because epidemiological evidence simply does not exist. Incidences of agranulocytosis may not be reported, or they may be reported as something else. Infections that eventually cause death are not always traced back to the anemia that brought them on.

While figures on the continuing effects of aminopyrine and dipyrone have not been compiled* the evidence of disease and death in the United States and elsewhere has not stopped the sale of aminopyrine and dipyrone to consumers who unknowingly become guinea pigs in a massive experiment in drug safety. In Brazil, dipyrone is sold over the counter. The prescribing guide issued for African physicians lists thirty-one preparations containing aminopyrine or dipyrone, recommended as "analgesics for minor conditions."[8] Packages of aminopyrine

---

*Sterling Winthrop (which manufactures dipyrone in Colombia for distribution throughout Latin America) and other multinational manufacturers of dipyrone contend that Latin American and Mediterranean people are less susceptible to agranulocytosis than northern Europeans, and they cite studies that show low reported incidences of the disease in Brazil, Israel, and Greece.[50]

and dipyrone products purchased in Thailand contained inserts claiming the products were "well tolerated," although they warned that in "rare cases" the products "may cause allergic reactions that necessitate discontinuation of the medicine."[20] Similar inserts have been found in packages of Avafortan, a product of Asta-Werke AG of West Germany ("a wide margin of safety") and Buscopan Compositum, made by another West German firm, Boehringer Ingelheim, ("Safety has been proven and confirmed in over 500 publications throughout the world").[8] The International Organization of Consumer Unions studied the *Drug Index for Malaysia and Singapore,* and found nineteen products containing dipyrone recommended for relatively minor ailments, including fever, headache, lumbago, and pains due to colds and flu.[17]   In most of those conditions, aspirin would be just as effective.[20]

### PRODUCTS CONTAINING DIPYRONE AS SOLE OR IN COMBINATION

| Trade Names | Manufacturer | Country found |
|---|---|---|
| Conmel | Sterling-Winthrop (USA) | Colombia, Malaysia, Singapore [17] |
| Bonpyrin | Takeda (JPN) | Malaysia, Singapore [17] |
| Novalgin | Hoechst (FRG) | Malaysia, Singapore [17] |
| Nominfone | Atlantic (USA) | Malaysia, Singapore[17] |
| Benza D, Benza Forte | Takeda (JPN) | Malaysia, Singapore[17] |
| Nomin | Atlantic (USA) | Malaysia, Singapore[17] |
| Dolo Adamon | Asta Werke | Malaysia, Singapore[17] |
| Dolo Neurobin | Merck-Zuellig (FRG) | Malaysia, Singapore[17] |
| Nomibar | Atlantic (USA) | Malaysia, Singapore[17] |
| Solovin | Takeda (JPN) | Malaysia, Singapore[17] |
| Cibalgin | Ciba-Geigy (SWTZ) | Monzambique, India[20] |
| Avafortan | Asta Werke (FRG) | Africa[8] |
| Buscopan Compositum | Boehringer Ingelheim (FRG) | Africa[8] |

Even drugs that are not harmful in and of themselves can indirectly endanger the lives and health of people who live in developing nations. A person suffering from cancer in Bangladesh, for example, might have read a newspaper adver-

tisement that proclaimed he could be cured by Cee Nu capsules*
and promptly made a trip to the nearest pharmacy — there
would be no need to stop at a physician's for a prescription
— to purchase the capsules.[12] What the shopkeeper and the
advertisement would not tell him, of course, is that Cee Nu is
hardly a cure for cancer, at least not by itself, although it is
used in combination with other drugs in chemotherapy programs.[60] Physicians in the United States are warned against
administering Cee Nu more frequently than at six-week inter-
vals, and when they prescribe Cee Nu, they keep a close watch
on the patient's liver function, because the drug can cause liver
problems and should not be used by people with liver disorders.
Unfortunately, our hypothetical Bangladeshi cancer patient
and his all-too-real counterparts not only mistakenly believe
their cancers cured, but also, in all likelihood, expose themselves
to more risk in taking the drug than would citizens of the industrial world. Medical authorities estimate that half the
population of Bangladesh suffers from some form of parasitic
disease or other liver disorder.[49] And chances are slim that any
of them consulted a doctor before or after taking Cee Nu.

**The Double Standard**

It is the same with regard to pharmaceuticals as for
pesticides: "Unsafe here — OK anywhere else." And the same
question applies. Are there truly circumstances in developing
countries which justify the widespread use of unproved or
hazardous drugs in spite of risks that citizens of the industrialized nations consider unacceptable? Many health professionals
join the pharmaceutical manufacturers in answering "yes" in
the case of Depo-Provera, a synthetic hormone-based contraceptive which, after being injected into a muscle, is released slowly into the woman's bloodstream, where it acts to suppress
ovulation and thereby prevent pregnancy for three to six
months after each injection. Depo-Provera is manufactured by
the United States-based Upjohn Company and its subsidiary

---

*Such an advertisement would be illegal in the United States, where truth in adver-
tising laws require "a true statement of the effectiveness of the drug for the selected
purposes for which the drug is recommended or suggested in the advertisement." (CFR
Title 21 Sect. 202-1) There is no such thing as over-the-counter chemotherapy for cancer
in the United States. Chemotherapeutic agents are available by prescription, or in the
course of hospital treatment. Cee Nu may be used in combination with other drugs
for relief of, but not as a cure for, cancer.

in Belgium. Women choose Depo-Provera injections for contraception in a number of European nations — West Germany, France, Belgium, Denmark, the Netherlands, and Switzerland [70] as well as in the developing nations. The debate centers on a 1978 decision by the U.S. Food and Drug Administration not to allow Depo-Provera to be used for contraception by American women, although it may be used in treating cancer of the uterine lining. That decision affected Third World countries which had been receiving most of their supplies of Depo-Provera under the auspices of the U.S. Agency for International Development because the agency's policy does not allow it to provide its clients — in this case, family planning agencies in the developing nations — with products not allowed for use by United States citizens. Since AID is the major source of American family planning assistance abroad, and since most of the family planning agencies served by AID cannot afford to purchase Depo-Provera on their own, the FDA decision amounted to a cutoff of supplies.

Those who favor continued distribution of Depo-Provera in developing nations come armed with emotional arguments about the critical problems of overpopulation, with attendant malnutrition, poverty, and disease — and about the appalling numbers of women dead or butchered as a result of childbearing or illegal abortion. They question the validity and sufficiency of the data that led the FDA to ban Depo-Provera as a contraceptive. The head of the Bangladesh family planning program charges "cultural imperialism."[76]

"The real point," says Dr. Douglas H. Huber of Johns Hopkins University School of Medicine, who practiced medicine for four years in Bangladesh, "is that a U.S. government agency cannot decide what is acceptable to the rest of the world. . . It is important to distinguish unethical marketing from the informed decisions of Third World countries that believe that a US regulatory agency's position is in error or is inappropriate for their countries. The large body of world opinion in disagreement with the FDA's position should foster respect for other countries' informed decisions to use Depo-Provera."[75]

The case against Depo-Provera in the United States includes studies on beagle dogs, showing an increased incidence of breast tumors associated with the drug; the possibility of fetal deformity when Depo-Provera fails and pregnancy occurs; FDA officials' doubts that Upjohn's proposed cancer study following Depo-Provera release, would produce meaningful data; the ready availability of alternative contraceptive methods, equally effective and in many cases safer; and a high incidence, affecting 91 percent of users, of menstrual irregularities,[21] including 59 percent who stop menstruating altogether. On the other side of the risk-benefit ledger, Upjohn officials say, no serious illness has been associated with Depo-Provera use among women who participated in fifteen years of clinical studies, and "[N]o deaths have been ascribed to Depo-Provera after more than fifteen years of safe, effective, and responsible experience throughout the world."[60]

"No one should pass final judgment until they have listened to and worked with the women of the developing world themselves," wrote Indian obstetrician and gynecologist Poura P. Bhiwandiwala in response to an article in *Mother Jones* titled "The Charge: Gynocide; The Accused: The U.S. Government."[71]   Dr. Bhiwandiwala, who is conducting studies in Thailand and Indonesia with women who have used Depo-Provera for at least ten years, says Third World women choose Depo-Provera because it is a convenient and reliable contraceptive, preferable by far to the much greater risks of death in childbirth or at the hands of an abortionist. She concludes, "[T]he use of every new drug is an experiment on our own species. This is the reality we have to live with. I cannot prove that Depo-Provera is completely safe to use, but in my judgment as a physician, I can say that, based on the evidence we currently have, it is reasonable to make it available. In the first ten years of its use, its safety record may be better than that of the Pill."[71]

Do Third World women's special needs for convenient and unobtrusive birth control methods justify the risks, whatever those risks may be, of Depo-Provera? And is their choice of contraceptive methods truly based on full awareness of the benefits and risks of various methods? An AID advisory committee of physicians and epidemiologists recommends that the agency change its policy and provide Depo-Provera in countries where it is requested, if those countries are notified of the drug's regulatory status in the United States, and if they are willing to educate women who may choose Depo-Provera and enroll them in follow-up studies. The debate undoubtedly will continue. Can the risk-benefit ratio of a drug vary from country to country, or is the manipulation of ratios simply an excuse for second-rate drug standards in the developing world? Can the women of developing nations properly weigh the risks and benefits of a drug about which even physicians disagree, especially in light of the consistent inadequacy of drug labeling and packaging in developing nations? Is their consent to be injected with Depo-Provera given freely or under pressure from clinic staffs? There are no easy answers.

If the ethical distinctions blur in the case of Depo-Provera, however, they remain quite sharp when applied to another class of medicines — antibiotics — described by Dr. Milton Silverman, lecturer in pharmacology at the University of California's Schools of Pharmacy and Medicine in San Francisco and author of *The Drugging of the Americas,* as among the most misprescribed of drugs.

Antibiotics are often called "wonder drugs" because they have played a dramatic role in reducing the number of deaths from diseases caused by microbes, and because they have made possible today's sophisticated heart and lung surgery (before antibiotics were available, patients were much more likely to die from infections following surgery).[79] But where antibiotics are sold over the counter and recommended indiscriminately for minor ailments as well as for life-threatening diseases, even miracle drugs cause problems. Some antibiotics have dangerous side effects. And when an antibiotic is over-used — that is, taken to relieve a variety of ailments for which other treatment would be sufficient — there is always the danger that bacteria will develop resistance, rendering the antibiotic useless. This danger is increased in the case of "combination" antibiotics — two or more antibiotics mixed and sold in fixed proportions. The mixtures cause even higher resistance rates because both drugs are automatically over-used, rather than just the one. Furthermore, "combination" antibiotics are generally unnecessary, since the physician can always prescribe his or her own "tailor-made" combination, if needed. In developing nations, where infectious diseases are a major public health pro-

48    PILLS, PESTICIDES & PROFITS

blem, the loss of an antibiotic as a tool in fighting disease is
a serious problem.

One of the best examples of misprescribed antibiotics is
chloramphenicol, a powerful drug still used to combat typhoid
fever and other whole-body infections caused by bacteria of the
family called Salmonella.[17, 20, 34, 37, 60]

Chloramphenicol was at one time used in the treatment of
general urinary tract and other infections, but shortly after its
introduction in 1947, doctors discovered that a few patients
who took the drug experienced severe, sometimes fatal side effects: an irreversible bone-marrow depression leading to aplastic
anemia, a class of diseases (agranulocytosis is one) in which
the bone marrow fails to produce adequate blood cells, red or
white, and which may leave the patient vulnerable to a whole
range of infections. Although only one of every 30,000 patients
treated with a single dose of chloramphenicol eventually
develops aplastic anemia, the percentage rises among patients
who take the drug more than once — a typical practice in
developing countries — and patients who develop aplastic
anemia often die. Those who recover frequently suffer from
acute leukemia, a cancer of the blood.[60]

Because of the danger of blood disease, chloramphenicol is
severly restricted in the United States. *The Physician's Desk
Reference* carries this warning, boxed and in bold-face type,
with the listing for Parke-Davis's chloramphenicol product,
Chloromycetin: "It must not be used in the treatment of trivial
infections where it is not indicated as in colds, influenza, infections of the throat, or as a prophylactic agent to prevent
bacterial infections."[60]

That warning contrasts sharply with the information given
about chloramphenicol products (Chloromycetin, McKesson's
Cloramfenicol MK, Boehringer's Chlopranficina, Beacons's
Beaphenicol, and others) contained in prescribing guides available in Malaysia and Singapore and in Latin America.[17, 37] In
the prescribing guide for Malaysia and Singapore, Chloramphenicol is recommended for "typhoid and paratyphoid fever,
gastrointestinal tract (G.I.T.) and urinary tract infec-
ons . . . respiratory infections, pertussis . . . viral, rickettsial
and bacterial infections . . . severe infections including typhoid
fever, enteric infections, ocular and aural infec-

tions."[17] Winifred Amene of the University of Nigeria Teaching Hospital wrote of chloramphenicol being used to treat minor infections there and at the military hospital where she had previously worked: "We even had a large stock of the syrup for infants."[34]

The rationale for continued use of chloramphenicol in the developing nations, according to Jay Kingham, vice president of the Pharmaceutical Manufacturers Association International Division, is that, in the absence of sophisticated diagnostic techniques, a patient stands a better chance of recovery if he is treated with a powerful antibiotic known to be effective against a wide variety of infection-causing organisms than if he is treated with a drug which may be safer but also useful against a narrower range of organisms.[46] A layman's translation might run something like this: If you don't know what is wrong with the patient, give him medicine that will work against as many diseases as possible, and you might get lucky and cure whatever it is he has.

One of the doctors who disputes that view is Paul Edelson, assistant professor of pediatrics and a specialist in infectious diseases at Harvard Medical School who has worked in Southeast Asia. Typhoid fever is generally not difficult to diagnose, he maintains, and in some countries, lay health workers have been readily taught how to recognize the disease. Even if safer drugs than chloramphenicol were not available for typhoid patients, he says, it still would not be necessary to use the drug so promiscuously.[77]

If a one-in-thousands chance of serious complications among patients taking chloramphenicol were the drug's only drawback, widespread use might have more defenders. But there is another potential problem, common to all antibiotics but dramatically demonstrated in Mexico in a case involving chloramphenicol, with even greater potential to cause human suffering and death. When antibiotics are used widely to treat minor illnesses, resistant bacterial strains emerge in the same way that insect strains become resistant to pesticides. Later, when the resistant bacteria strike, antibiotics can prove useless to combat disease.

In 1972, an epidemic of typhoid broke out in Mexico. In seven Mexico City hospitals alone, more than 3,500 cases were reported that year. Early in the epidemic, more than one of every eight patients died.[74] The epidemic was caused by chloramphenicol-resistant *Salmonella typhi* bacteria — but that was not recognized until hundreds of patients who had been treated with chloramphenicol (then still the drug of choice for typhoid fever) had failed to respond to the treatment, and died. Later studies showed that 96 percent of the *S. typhi* bacteria strains isolated in early 1972 were resistant to chloramphenicol. When the problem was finally recognized, doctors began to treat typhoid patients with another antibiotic, ampicillin, and a much greater percentage recovered. The epidemic subsided, with 814 cases of typhoid reported in the seven hospitals in Mexico City in 1973 and 204 in 1974.[74]

People continue to die because doctors, acting in good faith, treat them with drugs to which disease-causing bacteria have become resistant. Seven years after the Mexican typhoid epidemic, a BBC radio interviewer went to Bangladesh and found Combiotic, a combination of two antibiotics (streptomycin and penicillin) made by Pfizer, sold over the counter.

"What is this for? For which diseases?" he asked a shopkeeper. "Any disease," he was told. "No problems with this?" he asked. "No."[28]

The problems, in fact, are several. Streptomycin and penicillin should not be bottled together in the first place, according to a physician in Bangladesh, Zafrullah Chowdhry. "Every textbook says don't do it, every pharmacology book will say don't do it . . . . Here Combiotic is one of the big sells."[28] Because of the big sell, says Dr. Martin Schweiger, medical advisor and administrator of the Rangpur-Dinajpur (Bangladesh) Rehabilitation Service Health Program, Combiotic has caused a resistance problem:

"There's a high incidence of TB [tuberculosis] in the community. Streptomycin is a front-line drug for the treatment of tuberculosis. If patients have been, as they are, being exposed to streptomycin when they are in the pre-clinical phase of tuberculosis, it means that the tuberculosis, when it develops clinically, will be untreatable by one of the main-line drugs. Patients are very likely to die as a result of this. Bangladesh is not rich enough to start rushing into all the second-line drugs because the first one has been wasted."[28]

In 1978, Bangladesh announced plans to ban combinations of penicillin and streptomycin.[28] Other combination antibiotics, however, continue to cause problems, in Bangladesh and throughout the developing world. For example, Albamycin T, an Upjohn product also known as Panalba, combines novobiocin and tetracycline, and it sells freely in Brazil and Costa Rica, although in the United States it has been banned for more than a decade because one-fifth of the patients who took it had an allergic reaction, sometimes serious or even fatal.[49] The rationale given for use of combination-type antibiotics is that two drugs have a broader spectrum of action — that is, they kill more types of bacteria; that two antibiotics reinforce each other, and that a combination can be effective even if the organism is resistant to one component.[75] But there is little clinical evidence to back up the rationale.

"Simultaneous administration of antibiotics may be rational in some severely ill patients, but then the doses should be chosen individually," concluded two Swedish physicians who studied the marketing of obsolete combination antibiotics in Central America.[82] Many "irrational and possibly dangerous combinations" are still available there, the researchers reported.

Of the World Health Organization's list of 210 essential drugs, published to provide a basis for rational drug use in developing countries, where as much as 40 percent of the health-care budget may be spent on drugs, only sixteen are antibiotics. Yet the Swedish physicians, Lars L. Gustafsson and Katarina Wide, found more than two hundred antibiotic products sold in some Central American nations.

"How can doctors in these circumstances become familair with the essential properties of these important drugs?" they asked. "A simple reduction in the number of drugs might improve antibiotic use in clinical practice."[75]

In the summer of 1981, more than 150 physicians and scientists from twenty-five nations joined in signing a statement calling for international controls to halt the indiscriminate dissemination and use of antibiotics.[11,78] Warning that "unless steps are taken to curtail the present situation, we may find a time when such agents [antibiotics] are no longer useful to combat disease," the statement called for efforts to prevent infectious diseases through sanitation and personal hygiene, and to warn consumers, prescribers, dispensers, manufacturers, and government regulatory agencies of the dangers of antibiotics misuse. "Only then," the scientists concluded, "can we begin to institute measures to curb the unnecessary use and flagrant misuse of these drugs."

### MORE PROBLEM DRUGS

| Drug | Problems | Third World Notes |
| --- | --- | --- |
| Tetracyclines (antibiotics) | Can cause kidney or liver damage, should not be used by pregnant women, can cause defects in teeth and bones, should not be taken by children under 8.[58] | Commonly prescribed or sold OTC, without labels to warn consumers of potential problems. Forty tetracycline products available in Malaysia and Singapore are marketed without cautionary listings. Physicians' reference books in Mexico, Central America, Brazil, Argentina[17] do not discuss potential dangers. (Lederele, Dow Lepetit, Dumex, Pfizer.) |
| Lincomycin Hydrochloride (antibiotic) | Potentially toxic. Should be used only in the treatment of serious infections when penicillin is not appropriate.[41] | A promotional leaflet distributed in Brazil claims that Lincomycin hydrochloride is effective "for the immediate control of bacterial complications of the common cold, such as tonsillitis, otitis, bronchitis and pneumonia..." (Upjohn)[41] |
| Chloroform (anaesthetic) | Not approved for use in pharmaceutical products in the U.S. Toxic to liver.[49] Possibly carcinogenic. Banned in Canadian, German, Filipino pharmaceutical products.[17] | Still available in Malaysia and Singapore.[17] (Various manufacturers) |
| Oxyphenisatines (laxatives) | Incriminated in cases of liver injury. U.S. FDA approval withdrawn 1972, "not safe for use under the conditions of use for which they had originally been approved."[81] Withdrawn by Australia, Germany, Canada.[17] | "Prutabs" for chronic and habitual constipation still marketed in Malaysia and Singapore by Unichem.[17] |

MORE PROBLEM DRUGS *continued*

| Drug | Problems | Third World Notes |
|------|----------|-------------------|
| *Phenacetin* (analgesic) | Many cause serious anemias (blood disorders), kidney failure.[49] | In Malaysia, advertised for pain or depession. (Roche)[49] (Burroughs, Wellcome Wallace, SKF, Sandoz) |
| *Phenformin* (drug used to treat diabetes) | Removed from U.S. market 1978. Can cause fatal lactic acidosis. "Probably very few, if any, patients who cannot be managed by other therapeutic measures require phenformin." A.M.A.[58] | Marketed in Malaysia[17] by Hoescht. |
| *Verdivitone* (vitamin) | Contains about 17% alcohol.[43] Should not be used by patients with liver problems. Limited use in Britain.[49] | Sold OTC in Bangladesh, for "giving vitality, energy."[49] Half of Bangladesh's population suffers from amoebic hepatitis or some other liver disease. Many are Muslims, who are forbidden to use alcohol. (Squibb)[49] |

## Let the Traveler Beware

Carol Gates is a British woman who became ill with malaria while in Mozambique. She was given a course of antibiotics, and the malaria subsided, but she continued to feel tired and uncomfortable, and had recurring headaches. So she went to a pharmacy and bought some Cibalgin, a painkiller sold over the counter in Mozambique. (It is manufactured by Ciba-Geigy.) What she didn't know when she took the tablets — about eighteen altogether, she estimates — was that Cibalgin contains aminopyrine, one of the compounds withdrawn from the market in the United States and several European countries because of their association with serious blood disorders.

"They seemed to work," she said. "They killed the pain. And then after a few days I began to vomit and I had a very, very sore throat and the headaches came back and I had toothache." She went to the hospital, where she was given antibiotics and told to rest in bed for a few days. A doctor visited her two or three times a day, prescribing still another course of antibiotics while tests were conducted.

"At the end of a week," she said, "I couldn't walk and I couldn't talk because the whole of my mouth was covered with sores. I couldn't swallow, I also couldn't chew anything." After she had been hospitalized for two or three days, her baffled doctors sent her to another hospital for more tests. She remained there for five weeks. Her illness was eventually diagnosed as a secondary infection, brought on by her weak and defenseless condition, which had been caused by taking Cibalgin.

"It's something I shan't forget," she told an interviewer. "I had . . . blood poisoning . . . . and huge red lumps all over my body which were very sore . . . [I]t was painful even lying . . . The pain in my gums which were rotting, and my teeth, which were dying, was something I had never suffered before . . . I also had a lung infection and at one point my kidneys were functioning very badly. I was lucky they were able to treat it before my kidneys collapsed."[44]

Carol Gates was left with scars, and she feared she might lose her teeth, all because of a headache remedy. But in the end, she was indeed lucky. She survived. Other aminopyrine users have died from agranulocytosis and from infections brought on during drug-induced anemias.[20]

Ciba-Geigy and Sandoz, the Swiss multinational corporations that marketed aminopyrine, announced in 1977 their intention to replace aminopyrine in their products with another, safer painkiller. But Cibalgin products containing aminopyrine and manufactured as late as 1980 have been purchased, over the counter, in India and in other countries.[45]

## When Drugs Are Not The Answer

Two questions need to be considered in the discussion of pharmaceutical exports. One is whether the exported products meet the same standards of safety and effectiveness imposed on products manufactured for use in most industrial nations. We have seen that there are cases when they do not. An equally important question is whether the exported pharmaceutical products, even those acknowledged to be safe, are appropriate to the health care needs of the developing world. Often, again, they are not. The patterns of disease of the developing nations are different from those of the industrial world. The research divisions of major multinational pharmaceutical companies, as well as government-sponsored researchers in the industrial nations, devote most of their time and budgets to the development of drugs and vaccines for diseases that occur primarily in the developed world. In the United States, for example, of a biomedical research budget of $4.5 billion in 1977, only slightly more than 1 percent ($60 million) was spent on diseases of the developing nations.[65]

The reasons are primarily economic. Development of a single new drug can cost $30 to $60 million. Many Third World countries, particularly in South America, do not acknowledge patents, which leaves a company that invested heavily in developing a new drug vulnerable to "piracy" as soon as the drug is introduced.[65] And new drugs developed for tropical parasitic diseases, notes Dr. Harold J. Simon, professor of community medicine and director of international health programs at the University of California, San Diego School of Medicine, "would presumably be intended mostly for use in poor countries. Little direct financial return is to be expected from markets in the developing countries, and not very much from markets in the United States and other industrialized countries."[65]

The pharmaceutical industry, of course, does not exist for chiefly humanitarian reasons. Its interest is commercial, and it cannot be expected to devote its resources to ventures with little promise of return. Many of the health problems of the Third World require social, rather than chemotherapeutic, solutions. The diseases of poverty — malnutrition, parasitic infections, pneumonia, diarrhea, tuberculosis, leprosy — are unlikely to be conquered unless poverty itself is conquered. Indeed, vaccines and therapeutic drugs have been developed for the treatment of some of these diseases, but they may not be accessible to people in remote or rural areas who may need them most, either because the drugs are too expensive or because there is no health-care-delivery system.[65]

Still, the industry is not entirely without blame in the continuing high incidence of diseases typical to the developing world. Those nations' health care funds are limited, and they are spent largely for drugs. About 40 percent of the typical developing nation's health care budget goes for drugs, as op-

posed to 10 to 20 percent in developed countries.[11, 16, 20, 28, 75]
Several researchers have attributed the discrepancy at least
partially to demand created by the promotional activities of
drug companies.[20] And where mass-marketed drugs serve to
mask the true nature of public health needs or to provide a
panacea with little lasting effect, the pharmaceutical companies
bear responsibility for earning their profits at the expense of
people whose health care needs will remain unfulfilled.

## Whose Fault?

Pharmaceutical products pose two separate classes of problems
in the developing world. One is the availability of drugs known
to cause serious, life-threatening side effects. The second, much
more difficult to trace back to its sources, is the widespread
misuse of drugs which are not necessarily dangerous in and
of themselves but become so when taken without proper precautions. In the first case it is easy to blame the pharmaceutical
manufacturers and governments of exporting and importing
countries who knowingly distribute or allow to be distributed
products that endanger human health. In the second, however,
the finger of blame points in several directions. In the absence
of international controls on the distribution and use of pharmaceutical products, the only effective and available means for
keeping powerful drugs in trained hands may be educational
efforts to alert consumers to the benefits of preventive
measures and the hazards of relying on drug companies and
shopkeepers for accurate information about medicines.

Although each of the industrialized nations has a unique
regulatory scheme for ensuring the safety of pharmaceutical
products sold within its boundaries, the basic regulatory
elements are similar:

Pre-marketing evidence of quality, safety, and effectiveness;

Post-marketing surveillance to ensure continued quality, safety,
and effectiveness;

Requirements for accurate and truthful drug advertising and
labeling;

Requirements that new data about the drug is quickly made
available to physicians and regulatory authorities;

Means for removal from the market or restriction of a drug,
should new data warrant.[54]

The United States, which enacted one of the earliest pieces
of drug legislation in the world, the Pure Food and Drug Act
of 1906, now has one of the most stringent premarketing review
processes in the world. It requires a battery of tests first on
animals, then on healthy individuals, and finally on individuals
for whom the drug was developed.[54] Approval of a new drug
can take three to ten years or longer. But "approved for use
in the United States of America" is not necessarily a blanket
assurance for importing countries that a drug is safe. Many,
even most, of the drugs mentioned in this chapter are approved for limited use — against life-threatening illnesses, for terminally ill patients, or in cases for which no safer remedy is
available. Often those restrictions fail to accompany the products to their destinations. The reasons for this, and some sug-
gestions about what might be done to control the situation,
become apparent in a survey of the parties involved: the pharmaceutical companies that manufacture the drugs, the governments that regulate or fail to regulate them, the physicians who
prescribe them, the pharmacists or shopkeepers who dispense
them, and the consumers who take them.

Pharmaceuticals is among the most profitable of industries.
Sales of the top hundred companies were more than $48 billion
in 1977. [27] Exports have accounted for a growing proportion
of their sales. The International Federation of Pharmaceutical
Manufacturers' Associations estimated that in 1977, the "free
market" economies spent $39 billion on drugs, and developing
nations an additional $9 billion, or roughly 20 percent of the
total.[30,73] Multinational companies may have as many as fifty
foreign subsidiaries that are not controlled by the regulations
of the company's home country. These companies control a
large share of the pharmaceutical market in developing nations
and often serve as the major source of drug information for
doctors and pharmacies. Their sales are in some cases larger
than the gross national products of importing countries, with
obvious implications for the ability of the importing nations

to regulate them. The companies have often taken advantage of developing nations' inability to regulate their products. Products not approved in the United States and other industrial countries (for example, dipyrone) are manufactured for export by unregulated subsidiaries in the Third World. Products whose approval is withdrawn by the United States or another country are sometimes "dumped" in developing countries. Labeling is inconsistent; a product which carries a warning in one nation may not come packaged with the same warning elsewhere. The drug industry has maintained that the governments of developing nations should take more responsibility for enforcing consistent labeling requirements, and has made efforts recently in that direction. The IFPMA has drawn up a code of marketing practices, which the U.S. Pharmaceutical Manufacturers' Association has endorsed. Smithkline and French has centralized and standardized labeling for all international operations. Historically, however, the industry has not been successful at self-regulation; that is why developed nations have enacted their stringent regulations. And there is reason to doubt the industry's eagerness to initiate change. Although Ciba-Geigy's director of pharmapolicy, for one, claims that the industry would welcome an international, uniform set of regulations for each drug, because such a code would reduce the costs of dealing with separate regulatory agencies throughout the world, neither his company nor any other has suggested such a plan.[49]

Although accurate information on available drugs makes a physician's job easier, the task of choosing among thousands of brand-name drugs the remedy appropriate for an individual patient is still a difficult one.[27,55] In the developed nations, physicians usually have access to a number of sources of information about the recommended uses, contraindications, and side effects of various products — medical journals and libraries, consultation with other physicians, continuing medical education programs, prescribing guides such as *The Physician's Desk Reference*, American Medical Association drug evaluations, and information from drug company salesmen or "detailmen."[19,36] But in the Third World, the physician's access to information is often much more limited, especially for family practitioners without access to major medical centers.

Often these doctors rely heavily on two sources of information: the drug company "detailmen," who often outnumber a nation's physicians in a given nation, and prescribing guides such as *The Physician's Desk Reference,* which are in reality collections of paid advertisements by drug companies that choose which products to list.[37] In the developing nations, where truth-in-advertising laws may not exist or apply to drug advertisements, the prescribing guides, as illustrated by quotations throughout this chapter, do not always tell the whole story about a particular drug.

The pharmacist plays a much more important role in drug dissemination and use in developing nations than in the United States and European countries. In areas where there are not enough doctors — a chronic problem in developing nations — the pharmacist may be the only health care professional available and becomes, in effect, the prescriber.[37,46,55] Most developing nations do not have the kinds of educational and licensing requirements that limit the practice of pharmacy in developed nations to qualified professionals, however. In Colombia, for example, Dr. Hitzig Berggrun estimates that there are about 7,000 licensed pharmacists, of whom only 1,500 graduated from pharmacy school. The remainder earned their licenses through apprenticeships of clerking or assisting.[37] When products are not properly labeled, the pharmacist is often none the wiser, and may, with all good intentions, pass on a product to an unsuspecting public.

In some cases the consumer may have no guidance whatsoever, because drugs normally available by prescription only in the industrial nations are sold as freely as aspirin in developing countries. In such a situation the consumer's only defense is his own knowledge, which may be, as we have seen, sorely deficient.

# CHAPTER IV
## INDUSTRIES, HAZARDOUS WASTES AND CONSUMER PRODUCTS

The hazards visited upon Third World residents by the industries of the developed world do not always come in the form of clearly dangerous goods, developed or produced in the United States and Europe and sold without regard to their hazards overseas. But there is a pattern. Western markets for particular goods may shrink — because of regulatory action in developed countries (for example, pesticides), or because of some other factor suppressing consumer demand (for example, tobacco products, infant formulas). When a Western market dwindles, the developing world provides a relatively untapped market to which promotional efforts can be switched to keep up sales and profits.

In the same manner, industries whose products remain in demand in the developed world, but whose processes or wastes are unacceptable there, have found relief in the Third World from many of the regulations that industrial nations have adopted to protect workers and communities. The governments of Sierra Leone, Nigeria, Liberia, Senegal, and Chile have been offered cash payments[20] (lucrative in Third World terms but representing, to the companies making the offers, only a small portion of what it would cost to dispose properly of their toxic wastes within the United States) to accept those wastes for essentially unregulated disposal. Manufacturers of asbestos products and benzidine dyes have moved their plants to Third World nations where jobs and income are welcomed, and where dangers to workers are largely overlooked. The products, as

61

well as the profits, make their way to the United States and Europe.

In short, the industrial cycle, from processing raw materials to manufacturing to sales and use by consumers, and disposal of waste by the manufacturer, is exportable in segments. And whenever one of those segments poses hazards that industrialized nations either consider unacceptable or choose to regulate in a manner that requires industry to incur substantial expense, we can look for that segment to appear in the Third World.

**Industrial Hazards**

In Ahmedabad, India, Shree Digvijay, Ltd. produces 50,000 tons per year of asbestos-cement pipe sheet in a factory that the giant American asbestos corporation Johns-Manville supplied with technical and engineering assistance. Johns-Manville owns some shares in Shree Digvijay, serves as its selling agent for exports to the Middle East and Africa, and supplies the company with raw asbestos fiber.[6]

Asbestos is a general name for a family of fibrous minerals, used in such products as construction materials and automotive brake linings, that emits a microscopic fibrous dust. Inhalation of this dust causes a lung disease, asbestosis, for which there is no cure, and whose major symptoms appear several years after the onset of exposure. Asbestos fibers also migrate throughout the body and cause a variety of cancers, such as cancer of the lung and cancer of the stomach. Mesothelioma (cancer of the lining of the lungs), very rare in the general population, has been found in asbestos workers and also in their families, who have been exposed to the asbestos dust on the workers' clothes. People who live near asbestos plants, some of whom played on asbestos waste dumps as children, have also been known to develop this rare cancer.[8]

Asbestos waste from the Shree Digvijay plant litters nearby neighborhoods. Children play on the waste dumps around their homes. Untreated wastewater is dumped into an open trench banked by piles of solid waste. Shree Digvijay's products carry no labels warning users of the hazards of asbestos dust, and no directions advising how to avoid creating hazardous dust when cutting and working with asbestos cement products.

Johns-Manville, which has been sued for billions of dollars by United States workers claiming that the company is responsible for their cancer and asbestosis, claims to maintain a policy of selling asbestos fiber only to customers who meet government regulations on asbestos exposure, or, in countries such as India without governmental regulations on asbestos exposure, only to those who practice "accepted industrial hygiene."[2]

Hindustan Ferodo, Ltd. is another Indian company manufacturing asbestos products. The company makes asbestos brake linings, clutch facings, and asbestos textiles. It is 74 percent owned by the dominant British asbestos company, Turner and Newall.[2]

Inside the plant, conditions resemble those in British factories of fifty years ago. Neither workers nor management personnel know about the hazards of asbestos, according to a former employee of the company. Even the simplest hygienic measures are not taken. Dust is swept up dry with a broom instead of a wet mop. Workers are given uniforms, but the same locker is used for both work and street clothes. The former employee reported that asbestos dust within the plant is "very visible, as dense as the dust in the air behind a bus on a dirt road in dry season . . . [W]orkers [in the dustiest areas of the plant] are supposed to wear respirators of the canister type. However, they generally avoid this, because they're not given any indication that this dust is extremely hazardous. As far as they know, it's just very unpleasant to breathe because it's so thick. . . The rest of the workers in the plant are given cloths that resemble surgical masks. [F]ew employees use these devices. Generally, unless the dust is really a nuisance, clogging up the nose and so forth, no face mask is worn. There are no notices anywhere in the plant warning against the dangers of excessive dust inhalation."[3]

Hindustan Ferodo workers are medically screened once or twice a year. They do not know the purpose of the chest x-rays they receive, nor are they told of the results. Conditons in the areas where asbestos waste from the overworked ventilation ducts is packaged are even worse than those inside the plant.

The waste is packed in jute bags that leak dust profusely. "Outside" contract laborers are used in this area, and they are given no respiratory protection, no uniforms, and no medical checkups. They are often covered with dust, white from head to toe.

Hindustan Ferodo's management asserts that the factory has a good medical record. The *Times of India* reported, however, that the company fired employees whose medical examinations revealed they were suffering from asbestosis. At least 35 percent of those still on the job at Hindustan Ferodo are afflicted by asbestos-related disease, but receive no compensation.[13]

India is not the only developing country in which asbestos companies with ties to the industrial world operate without adequate safeguards for their workers' health. Amatex, a firm based in Norristown, Pennsylvania, owns asbestos textile plants in the border towns of Agua Prieta and Ciudad Juarez, Mexico. Amatex "imports" asbestos textiles into the United States from its border plants. An Arizona newspaper reporter and an industrial health specialist, visiting the Agua Prieta plants, described conditions there:

> Asbestos waste clings to the fence that encloses the brick plant and is strewn across the dirt road behind the plant where children walk to school. Inside, machinery that weaves yarn into industrial fabric is caked with asbestos waste and the floor covered with debris. Workers in part of the factory do not wear respirators that could reduce their exposure to asbestos dust.[2]

A television crew from Texas visited the Juarez plant soon afterward. One worker, whose identity was concealed, said he had not been warned that he could develop a fatal disease from breathing asbestos dust. He described the lack of dust controls in the plant, and the lack of protective face masks or clothing. When the story about the unsafe conditions at the Amatex plant ran in the Juarez newspapers, several workers quit their jobs out of fear for their health.[14]

Asbestos plants in the developing world provide perhaps the clearest examples of the double standard that provides Western consumers with goods and corporations with profits at the expense of unspecting workers who are exposed to health and safety hazards that would not be tolerated in the countries that reap the fruits of their labors.

In the United States, workplace standards for asbestos exposure have been consistently tightened, from five million fibers per cubic meter of air to two million fibers. New recommendations as low as 100,000 fibers, which represents the lowest level of asbestos that can be readily monitored, are pending. There is probably an increased risk of cancer associated with even this level.[2] The federal Environmental Protection Agency is empowered to limit or even ban asbestos-containing wastewater discharge. Asbestos has been banned outright in products such as molded pipe insulation.[8] In other products, its use is being phased out as less hazardous substitute materials become available. Dr. Anthony Robbins, former Director of National Institute for Occupational Safety and Health (NIOSH) has said he knows of not one use in which substitutes for asbestos could not be developed.[5]

A combination of lack of regulations and lack of enforcement capability permits the vastly different situation in the Third World. Mexico, for example, has no specific regulations designed to protect asbestos workers. General workplace regulations require that posters be displayed warning workers of dangers to which they are exposed, and that adequate protective means be provided for the workers; the fine for failure to meet these requirements may not exceed one thousand pesos (US $45). South Korea has no health regulations for asbestos exposure at all. Taiwan has set a ceiling on asbestos dust (two milligrams per cubic meter of air) that essentially treats asbestos dust as little more than a nuisance.

Brazilian law provides for three levels of hazard pay: Asbestos brake shoe and asbestos cement manufacture are rated at the medium level of hazard, while asbestos textile manufacture is not rated as hazardous at all. Hazardous work thus becomes economically attractive, and improved working conditions bring pay cuts.[2]

As the U.S. asbestos industry has come under increasing regulation, imports from countries in which asbestos is poorly regulated have soared. From 1969 to 1976, overall U.S. imports of asbestos textiles nearly tripled, rising from three million to almost nine million pounds per year. Imports from

the relatively regulated country of Canada, which made up the
bulk of imports for 1969, declined slightly in 1970s; imports
from the less regulated countries of Mexico, Taiwan and Brazil,
virtually nonexistent in 1969, approached or exceeded the level
of Canadian imports by 1976.[12]

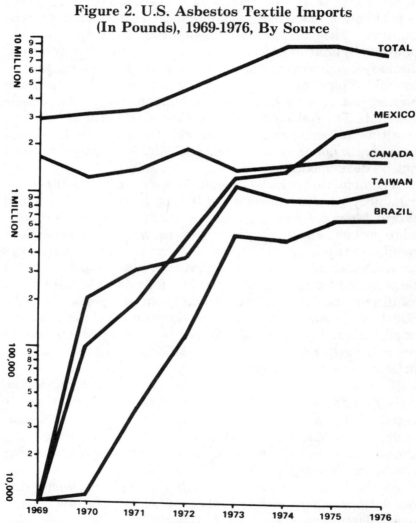

**Figure 2. U.S. Asbestos Textile Imports
(In Pounds), 1969-1976, By Source**

*Reprinted by permission from Barry I. Castleman, "The Export of Hazardous Factories to Developing Nations,"* The International Journal of Health Services 9, no. 4 (1979): p. 574.

Publicity about asbestos-related disease, combined with unfavorable economic conditions in general, precipitated a 34 percent drop in purchases of asbestos in the United States in 1980.[15] As consumers in other developed nations follow suit, the multinational asbestos companies look for new markets for their products in the developing world, where asbestos hazards are little understood and poorly regulated. Many plants, such as Hindustan Ferodo, serve as export bases and also supply domestic markets in the face of decreasing demand in developed countries and increasing demand in the Third World.[16]

Benzidine dyes are an example of a situation in which the developed world will no longer tolerate the process, but continues to import the product from industries that operate under substandard conditions in developing countries, thus subsidizing the hazardous industrial process.

Benzidine dyes are used mainly to color cotton textiles, paper, and leather. Benzidine has been linked to human bladder cancer since the early decades of this century, when the incidence of bladder cancer among benzidine workers was found to be many times greater than that of the general population. The Occupational Safety and Health Administration (OSHA) in the United States issued a workplace standard for benzidine in 1974.[17] In 1978 The National Institutes of Occupational Safety and Health (NIOSH) and the National Cancer Institute issued a warning that recommended that three benzidine dyes be handled as carefully as if they were benzidine itself. Health concerns led Sweden, England, Italy, Japan, and Switzerland to outlaw or abandon the manufacture of benzidine dyes.[2]

By 1976, only one small firm, Fabricolor, still manufactured benzidine dyes in the United States. Some former customers of benzidine dyes have stopped using them, but some have turned to foreign sources of the dyes.[2]

Imports have soared from 25,000 pounds in 1975 to more than 400,000 pounds in 1979.[17] France, Egypt, and India were the major suppliers. The substandard conditions in some of these foreign plants is attested to by the residual benzidine present in the imported dyes. Samples of imported dyes have, on the average, four times as much residual benzidine as the domestically produced dyes once had. One sample from Egypt of the most popular benzidine dye, Direct Black 38, contained sixty times as much unconverted benzidine.[7]

The export of hazardous industrial processes is not always directed at the Third World. The less regulated country vicitimized by a hazardous industry operating according to the double standard may be another developed country. Such is the case of the notorious Swiss-owned trichlorophenol plant that operated in Seveso, Italy.

On July 10, 1976, the chemical reaction used to make trichlorophenol went out of control at the Seveso plant. TCDD (2,3,7,8-tetrachlorodibenzo-p-dioxin), one of the most toxic substances ever synthesized by man and a contaminant of the process used to make trichlorophenol, was vented to the atmosphere. Seven hundred Seveso residents were evacuated from their homes, and some may never be able to return. Approximately 90 pregnant women exposed to TCDD, a potent teratogen (causing deformities in embryos and fetuses), underwent abortions.

The formation of TCDD in the process of making trichlorophenol is a recognized hazard. More TCDD is formed at high reaction temperatures. In the United States, plants such as the one at Seveso, have a heat control mechanism and a holding tank system as standard safety features to help prevent runaway reactions and to limit contamination should an explosion occur. In addition to the company's failure to equip the Seveso plant with these standard safety features, workers in the plant were not even told about the dioxin hazards. According to environmental consultant Barry Castleman, it is doubtful that Givudan Corporation, a subsidiary of the pharmaceutical giant Hoffmann-LaRoche, would be permitted to operate a trichlorophenol plant in Switzerland under the lax standards it used in Seveso.[2]

There are still more industries in which some companies observe a double standard in occupational or environmental protection, or both.

• In Managua, Nicaragua, more than a third of the workers at a chemical plant managed and partially owned by the Philadelphia-based multinational firm Electro-quimica Pennwalt have suffered from central nervous system damage caused by mercury poisoning. A Nicaraguan government official found puddles of mercury on the floor of the plant; workers, contrary to company claims, had not been informed of the dangers of mercury exposure, nor had they been provided with protective equipment. Pennwalt and the Nicaraguan government (as part owner) are sharing the cost of the plant's cleanup. Pennwalt settled out of court with four permanently disabled workers, agreeing to pay them lifetime pensions since they can no longer work.

The lakeside chemical plant threatened not only the health of the workers in the plant, but endangered the health of all residents of Managua as well. During its twelve years of operation, the plant discharged an estimated forty tons of mercury into Lake Managua, the city's source of drinking water and a major source of fish. The Nicaraguan government is considering various plans to clean up mercury from the lake's bottom, but may not be able to afford an extensive decontamination program.[18,19]

• The Malayawata steel mill has a reputation as the filthiest and most dangerous factory in Malaysia. Clouds of black smoke and iron dust are sucked into an overworked hood, and the rest rolls over the steelworkers and up through the roof. Laws protecting workers from exposure to hazardous chemicals are weaker in Malaysia than in Japan, where the Nippon Steel Corporation, builder and minority partner in the Malayawata mill, is based. What is more, the weak Malaysian laws are seldom enforced.[4]

### Hazardous Wastes

As the United States government has acted to impose strict regulations on the domestic transport and disposal of hazardous wastes, American companies have begun to seek solutions to their waste control problems in less regulated developing countries. Several nations in West Africa, the Caribbean, and Latin America have been approached, in some cases with lucrative offers of payments for receiving industrial wastes from the United States.

Most developing countries have neither government agencies, regulatory authority, nor technical expertise sufficient to prevent the occurence of "Love Canals" — sites where unsuspecting residents are exposed to hazardous chemicals improperly disposed of, such as the notorious one in upstate New York. Yet because no comprehensive United States or international laws govern the export and disposal on foreign soil of toxic wastes, the developing world must once again weigh the payoff, whether it is economic development or technical assistance or simply cash, against the risks to health and environment posed by toxic wastes.

Petroleum refineries, rubber, plastic, textile, chemical, and metal industries are among the major producers of hazardous chemical wastes. By U.S. Environmental Protection Agency (EPA) estimates, 35 to 50 million metric tons of these wastes are generated in the United States every year, and the volume is increasing.[22] Some of these wastes are products that could be recovered, reprocessed, and recycled, but most companies find it cheaper and easier to dispose of them instead. The EPA estimates that as much as 60 percent of the waste is liquid or sludge, as much as 90 percent of which is disposed of improperly — by storage in non-secure ponds, lagoons, or landfills, or by incineration without proper controls.[22]

Improper disposal of hazardous wastes threatens public health and the environment. These wastes are contaminating groundwater supplies upon which Americans depend for drinking water and irrigation. Already thousands of private and public wells throughout the United States have been closed because of contamination. Once contaminated, groundwater may never again be safe.

Since 1978, the United States has begun to develop stringent domestic regulations for the proper disposal of toxic wastes under the federal Resource Conservation and Recovery Act. Industries generating hazardous wastes and dumpsite operators are increasingly being held accountable for damages resulting from improper disposal. The legislation, however, left a tempting loophole by failing to deal with the matter of hazardous waste exports. Some company officials have been quite frank about their decision to use the loophole. Many companies have accumulated toxic wastes at manufacturing sites because they have been unable to find or are unwilling to finance suitable disposal sites. According to one company official, "[I]n foreign countries you don't have that fear."[31]

Few, if any, developing countries have the technical expertise or regulatory machinery to handle hazardous wastes. In fact, few *developed* countries do. Japan, the Federal Republic of Germany, and Canada have the only waste-recycling facilities capable of dealing with shipments from abroad, according to the U.S. State Department.[32] Governments of developing countries usually do not have facilities or staff to monitor the effects of hazardous wastes on their people's health and environment.

The first reported incident of attempts to export hazardous wastes followed quickly upon enactment of the Resource Conservation and Recovery Act. In October 1979, the State Department learned that Nedlog Technology Group of Arvada, Colorado, had offered President Shiaka Stevens of Sierra Leone "up to $25 million" in advance for permission to dispose of hazardous wastes from the United States in that small West African nation.[20] Details about how the waste was to be handled and processed, and explanations about the source of the multimillion-dollar payment, were sketchy, but the scheme apparently involved shipment of wastes to Pepal, a small port about thirty miles northwest of Freetown, Sierra Leone's capital. From Pepal, the wastes were to be sent by rail to the interior of the country for disposal.

Under pressure from his constituents and citizens of neighboring Nigeria and Ghana, as well as from the U.S. State Department, President Stevens in February 1980 rejected the plan as "fool-hardy."[34] This incident, however, was only the first of reported plans to ship toxic chemical wastes to the Third World. None of the subsequent proposals, once made public, met with much enthusiasm. None has been approved by the State Department or the developing country involved. Covert deals, however, may have met with more success.

Haiti, an impoverished island republic only about one and one-half times the size of New Jersey, was approached in 1980 with a proposal which, according to the U.S. Embassy there, clearly "sought to take advantage of the lack of expertise here in Haiti to deal with such matters."[26] James Joyce, a former Democratic chairman of Camden County, New Jersey, free pendng an appeal of a conviction for jury tampering, negotiated with Haitian officials for development of a landfill for toxic wastes from the paint industry in New Jersey. The plan, which ended with Joyce's death later that year, coincided with the adoption of strict new legislation governing the dumping of chemical wastes in New Jersey.

That same year, the Haitian government turned down a proposal for an extensive facility, not of toxic wastes but of municipal sewage sludge from Washington, D.C. Promoters then took the proposal to the Caribbean island nation of Antigua and were again turned down. The plan had the backing of the District of Columbia Sanitary Commission but provoked this response from the State Department: "[T]he image of . . . sending the wastes of the nation's capital to the most densely populated and poorest country in the Americas is something that is not very appealing. . . It's something that is bound to cause a lot of public resentment and criticism in the Third World."[28]

Another proposal to export hazardous wastes was soon made public. In November 1980, Ashvins USA, an Alabama firm which handles chemical waste from paint and pesticide manufacturing and electroplating companies, filed for incorporation with the State Department three days before strict federal controls on toxic waste disposal were to go into effect.[31,32] Ashvins was thus exempted from the controls, which apply only to companies formed *after* the law was enacted. In December, Ashvins informed the State Department of plans to locate a disposal site in the Bahamas.[32]

The Bahamas, like Sierra Leone and Haiti, has no waste processing facilities. Ashvins proposed to furnish technical expertise to the Bahamian company that would ultimately be in charge of disposal — but did not agree to accept liability for any damages from improper disposal. Indeed, avoiding U.S. regulations that make operators of hazardous waste disposal facilities liable in case of accident is one of the primary advantages of locating a disposal site in the Third World. Ashvins treasurer Ray Bass, asked about liability, responded: "Anybody can sue anybody. That question is up to the courts. I'm not an expert on international law, but I'm sure it would be more difficult to sue in a foreign country."[31]

Hazardous wastes have thus become a foreign relations as well as public health and environmental problem. The 1981 arrest by Mexican authorities of an American alleged to have imported toxic wastes from the United States to a dumpsite he owned and operated in Mexico is a case in point. The incident also points out the inadequacy of existing U.S. regulations and corporate policy to ensure the safety of foreign citizens.

In March 1981, the Mexican government informed the U.S. State Department of the arrest of Clarence Nugent, a 75-year-old United States citizen, charged with illegally importing hazardous wastes and violating Mexican health laws. Nugent had imported wastes from companies in Texas and Kentucky for disposal and incineration at a site which he operated in a small town in Mexico. Among the wastes in the shipment of February 27, 1980, for which Nugent was arrested, were seventeen drums containing highly toxic polychlorinated biphenyls (PCBs) from the Diamond Shamrock Corporation in Dallas, Texas.[33]*

Mexican officials said Nugent's actions were illegal under an official embargo on hazardous wastes and requested that the United States take responsibility for cleaning up the disposal site and returning the wastes to the United States.[36] They charged that Nugent had dumped as much as 5,000 tons of mercury cinders into the dry river bed and sold the empty containers to local people for water storage.[33] Spokesmen for the U.S. companies involved claimed that Nugent had assured them that he was authorized by the Mexican government to dispose of hazardous wastes and that he had the facilities to dispose of them properly.[33,36]

Incidents such as these in Mexico, the Caribbean, and Africa show that current regulations are not adequate to protect residents of the developing world from the dangers of hazar-

---

*PCBs are highly stable, toxic materials used as insulation in transformers, capacitators, and other electrical equipment. In the United States, the federal Toxic Substances Control Act specifically prohibits the production of PCBs, restricts the use of existing PCBs, and regulates the disposal of PCB-contaminated material. After May 30, 1980, PCBs could not be exported unless the receiving government sent the U.S. State Department a "memorandum of understanding" assuring the existence of safe disposal or incineration facilities. The export of four other chemicals — chlorofluorocarbons, dioxin, asbestos, and N-methanesulfonyl-P-toluenesulfonomide (MSTS) — is similarly regulated under the Act.*

dous wastes. Under the federal Toxic Substances Control Act, wastes containing significant quantities of PCBs, chlorofluorocarbons, dioxin, asbestos, or MSTS are subject to export restrictions, but all other toxic wastes may be exported, so long as the exporter notifies the Environmental Protection Agency of its intention, and so long as the notification is relayed through the U.S. State Department to the importing country.

State Department officials have been quite vocal in disapproving of the hazardous waste disposal schemes. Apparently smarting from public criticism of shipments of wastes from the United States to authorized disposal sites in Canada and West Germany, the department lost little time in intervening in subsequent deals proposed to developing countries. Beginning with the Sierra Leone incident, the department cabled United States embassies in approximately sixty developing countries that were potential candidates for hazardous waste disposal proposals, urging them to report approaches or contacts by companies in the hazardous waste disposal field.[37]

Although the Resource Conservation and Recovery Act requires companies seeking to establish disposal sites abroad to notify the State Department, deals in toxic wastes outside the law, without the knowledge of the governments involved, remain a possibility. In early 1980, before the news of waste shipments to Mexico became public, a Philadelphia landfill owner revealed to the *Washington Post* that he had obtained permission to start shipping wastes to an African coastal country, which he would not identify. The State Department knew nothing of the plan.[20]*

To date, there have been no known attempts by companies based outside the United States to ship toxic wastes to developing countries. But throughout the industrial world, dumping wastes into the ocean has been a popular proposal. Such plans threaten not only local, but also global contamination.

Recognizing the international scope of the hazardous waste disposal issue, the United Nations has taken some action. In 1980, the Governing Council of the United Nations Environ-

---

*As of October 1981,. a bill, the "Export of Hazardous Waste Control Act of 1981," which would require exporters to acquire validated licenses based on proof that the importing country had been adequately informed and consent obtained, had been introduced in the U.S. Senate but not acted upon.

mental Programme (UNEP) urged member states to develop appropriate notification procedures for the international shipment of wastes. In a subsequent meeting, the Council planned to evaluate guidelines for "safe and appropriate disposal of hazardous chemical wastes and pertinent measures concerning their transboundary transport."[34] UNEP's suggestion closely resembles a resolution adopted by the United Nations General Asssembly in 1979 urging the "exchange of information on hazardous chemicals and unsafe pharmaceutical products that have been banned in their territories and to discourage, in consultation with importing countries, the exportation of such products to other countries." These recommendations, however, remain strictly voluntary.


**Infant Formula**

Economic and social conditions in developing countries can make a normally harmless product hazardous. Infant formula, a product whose use is not regulated, and which is widely used and accepted in developed countries, is such a case. In developing countries, where facilities for formula's proper use are scarce or absent, misused infant formula can cause disease and even death. Estimates of infant deaths in the Third World traceable to diarrhea and malnutrition associated with infant formula misuse run as high as one million per year.[46]

Human milk has recognized advantages over infant formula. Even when formula is prepared with sanitary water and dispensed from sterilized bottles, its bacterial counts are higher than those of breast milk. Human milk contains substances which help immunize the child against disease. Chemicals known as immunoglobulins, present in the colostrum (first days of mother's milk), guard against certain infections, while helping to discourage the growth of harmful microorganisms in general.[42] Antibodies in breast milk also protect the child against bacteria that cause diarrhea,[38, 44] a life-threatening disease for Third World infants. Diarrhea interferes with nutrient absorption[42] and is thus associated with malnutrition. Acute diarrheal disease is the leading cause of death among adults as well as infants in eight Latin American countries,[39] and diarrheal disease is as much as ten times more frequent among non-breast-fed Mexican children than among the breast-fed.[40]

When mothers substitute infant formula for breast-feeding, they lose some of the psychological bonding benefits promoted by breast-feeding, as well as the natural contraceptive effect of lactation, which may be particularly significant in the developing world.[46] More threatening, however, poverty and unsanitary conditions make the use of infant formula dangerous. Often the only water available for mixing the formula is contaminated. Facilities for sterilizing bottles and refrigerating prepared formula are lacking. One study in rural Chile found widespread bacterial contamination of bottles and formula, indicating improper use.[39]

In the poorest countries, infant formula purchases can amount to 85 percent of a family's income.[47] Faced with such a huge expense, mothers often dilute the powder, stretching a four-day supply (one pound) to make it last as long as three weeks. A survey in Barbados found 82 percent of mothers who used infant formulas were overdiluting them.[48]

Mothers who are unable, for whatever reason, to breast-feed their children have a real need for formulas, and in that context, distributors of formulas provide an essential service. With proper hygienic facilities and educational programs to teach mothers the correct use of formula, the risks can be minimized. Whose responsibility is it, then, to assure that useful products are not converted to hazards, and to see that they are not used unnecessarily by consumers who thereby expose their children to inordinate risks of disease and death? Once again, we see a situation in which neither exporters nor importers have taken sufficient precautions.

Several multinational corporations based in the United States and Europe have played a major role in shifting the preference of mothers in developing nations from breast-feeding to the bottle. Three United States-based companies export infant formula: Abbott Laboratories (which produces Similac), American Home Products (SMA and S-26), and Bristol-Myers (Enfamil). The Swiss-based Nestlé company dominates the Third World infant formula market, with a 50 percent share.[49]

These companies, because of declining population growth rates and reduced demand for infant formula products in most developed countries, have been seeking new markets in developing nations.[42] They inaugurated Third World advertising campaigns in the 1960s, promoting infant formula as "modern" and belittling breast-feeding as "old-fashioned" and "inconvenient."[41] The graph below shows the decrease in breast-feeding that occured in four developing nations during the period that saw the first extensive promotion of formulas.[45]

## Figure 3. Decrease of breast-feeding in the Third World during the 1960s (in percentages).

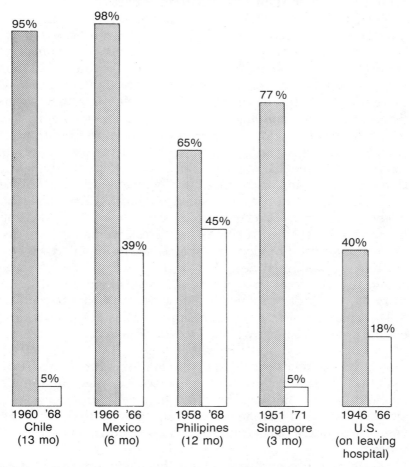

*Data from: Derrick B. Jelliffe and E. F. Patrice Jelliffe, "Human milk, nutrition, and the world resource crisis: Science 188 (9 May 1975): 557-61.*

Churches and other concerned groups have severely criticized the methods used in the Third World by multinational companies to promote infant formulas. Some of these companies have attempted, through advertising, to instill in Third World women a false belief that infant formula is more nutritious for their babies than breast milk, when experts agree that exactly the opposite is true.[50] Mass media campaigns also hint at the glamour of emulating Western ways. Formula advertisements show pictures of lovely, fat babies, usually Western, implying that formula makes these infants so much more robust than their Third World counterparts.[47]

Critics also attack the companies' practice of employing "milk nurses" to personally encourage new mothers to bottle feed. These professional nurses (or sometimes, untrained personnel in white nurse-like uniforms) are hired by infant formula makers, sometimes on a commission basis,[49] to persuade mothers to use infant formula. They visit maternity wards, distributing free samples and instructing the women in their use. (The brief lesson, however, does not guarantee that the women will use formula properly, since the water supply remains contaminated, facilities for sterilization and refrigeration are still lacking, and limited family income still necessitates that formula be diluted to make it last longer.) They influence women who might otherwise breast-feed their infants without incident to bottle-feed them instead. These women believe they are being advised by neutral medical professionals who have the infant's welfare at heart.[51] The "milk nurses" are often not recognized for what they are — saleswomen employed by the formula producers to develop markets for their products.

Distribution of free formula samples, besides encouraging emulation of Western ways, also may make bottle feeding a physical necessity. Mothers who postpone lactation while trying the free samples provided by "milk nurses" may experience real difficulties in attempting to breast-feed when the samples run out.[48] The mothers become "hooked" on breast milk substitutes, both psychologically and physically, and by the time the dangers to their infants posed by formula become apparent, they no longer have any choice in the matter.

Industry representatives claim that they aim promotional efforts at only those wealthy families able to afford and properly use infant formula. The desire among poorer mothers to imitate the upper classes is, they say, a purely unintentional side effect. Critics contend, however, that the number of wealthy families in developing countries is too small to constitute a profitable market, and that the multinational companies that produce infant formula deliberately aim their promotion toward the much greater population of poor women.[48]

Under pressure from groups outraged by their marketing practices in Third World countries, many infant formula makers have adopted self-regulatory codes of conduct. Critics characterize the self-imposed codes as weak, and even so, not always adhered to. Investigations in Africa revealed that United States-based multinationals were distributing bags advertising their products, and were making false nutritional claims about infant formula, both in violation of their own marketing codes. Hospital employees in Tanzania were given sizeable supplies of infant formula samples by a company representative, but they were not informed that the company's policy prohibited the distribution of free samples. In Kenya, brochures and containers in gift packs explicitly violated their distributor's code by failing to emphasize the superiority of breast feeding.[43]

Formula makers have used several strategies to counter the negative publicity received by their marketing practices in developing countries. Soon after concerned groups began boycotting Nestlé products in 1977 to protest that company's formula marketing, Nestlé retained a public relations firm to check the boycott. Failing in that effort, the company retained another agency in an attempt to undermine public sympathy of the boycott. A Nestlé vice-president wrote in a memo, subsequently "leaked:"

> The basic *strategy* for dealing with the boycott, i.e., containment of the awareness of the boycott campaign, without being ourselves responsible for escalating awareness levels, is working.

> It is clear that we have an urgent need to develop an effect[ive] counter propaganda operation, with a network of appropriate consultants in key centers, knowledgeable in the technicalities of infant nutrition in developing coun-

tries, and with the appropriate contact to get articles placed[52]

Nestlé also contributed $25,000 in 1980 to the Ethics and Public Policy Center, whose founder, Ernest Lefever, volunteered the organization for "additional activity" to further Nestlé's cause. (Lefever was nominated in 1981 to be Under Secretary of State for Human Rights, but his nomination was withdrawn when a storm of public protest broke out.) Throughout the public relations campaign, Nestlé refused to deal substantively with the charges leveled against the company.[32]

The Nestlé boycott was organized by the Infant Formula Action Coalition (INFACT) in 1977, and supported by health workers, churches, women's groups, and concerned individuals. The boycott was only a first step in an international grassroots campaign to stop irresponsible promotion of infant formula. In 1978, the World Health Assembly passed, for the second time in four years, a resolution urging member nations to take action to encourage breast feeding and discourage the high-pressure promotion of breast milk substitutes.[43] Representatives of governments, United Nations agencies, infant formula manufacturers, and citizens' groups met in Geneva, Switzerland, a year later, and agreed that such practices as advertising infant formula to the public, distributing free samples, and employing "milk nurses" should be stopped. Delegates also agreed that an international code of conduct on infant formula marketing should be established.[62] But those recommendations had little apparent effect on formula makers. The International Baby Food Action Network, a coalition of activist organizations, found that six months after the Geneva meeting, the multinational infant formula producers had violated the recommendations in more than two hundred incidents in thirty-three countries.[63]

The recommendations were adopted as an official international code of the World Health Organization for the marketing of infant formula in May, 1981, by a vote of one hundred eighteen to one, with the United States casting the dissenting vote.[53,54,55,56,57] The code is a voluntary one, meant to serve as guidelines for member states of the United Nations. It recommends that nations enact regulations on infant formula that:

- Outlaw advertising or other form of promotion to the general public;
- Prohibit the distribution of free samples to pregnant women and health-care workers, except for testing;
- Prohibit premiums to promote sales;
- Bar salesmen from getting in touch with mothers;
- Outlaw commissions on sales; and
- Prohibit product labels that idealize infant formula.[58]

United States officials, speaking for the administration of President Ronald Reagan, explained their dissenting vote in terms of disapproval of WHO's involvement in regulatory commercial codes, and in terms of the belief that the proposed restrictions on advertising would, if adopted, violate the First Amendment to the U.S. Constitution.[53]

The industry lobbied heavily against the WHO code, arguing that the code's provisions would interfere with free speech and trade.[58] Industry officials contend that the causal link between infant formula promotional techniques and Third World mothers' decisions not to breast-feed has not been fully established.[59]

Two officers of the U.S. Agency for International Development (AID) resigned in protest of the "No" vote. Dr. Stephen Joseph, the agency's highest-ranking health professional, deplored the tactics of infant formula makers in influencing the U.S. vote, noting that industry lobbyists "... have engaged in a systematic campaign of 'disinformation' intended to create a U.S. government position against the proposed code."[60] Responding to industry and administration charges that the provisions of the code would illegally restrain free speech and trade, Dr. Joseph likened the proposed actions to the warning labels required on cigarette packages, or the ban on flammable children's sleepwear. Major public health considerations must take precedence over proprietary rights, he said.[60]

Eugene Babb, who also resigned from AID, responded to the charge that the code was rigid and inappropriate international commercial regulation:

> This code has been a long time in the making and represents the hard work of many people, public and

private from many countries and international, agencies. There have been compromises on all sides to achieve a reasonable and balanced code which deals with the issues of breast feeding and marketing of infant formulas in a responsible manner. It respects the right of sovereign nations. The code is voluntary and will be used by each country according to their own desires, and consistent with their own laws and practices.[61]

Because of the voluntary nature of the code, independent actions by developing countries will determine its effectiveness in protecting the lives and health of infants from the inappropriate and hazardous use of infant formula. But there are signs of progress in this area. Even before the adoption of the WHO code, several Third World governments independently took action to regulate the marketing and sale of infant formula, or the bottles and nipples required for their use — countries such as Jamaica, Ghana, Algeria, Brazil, Colombia, Indonesia, Mexico, and Papua New Guinea.[46] Other countries have considered their own national legislation in the wake of the code's adoption.[41]

# CHAPTER V
# THE SEARCH FOR SOLUTIONS

The nations of the world have long been concerned about the dangers posed by toxic substances and hazardous products. Since the beginning of this century, many countries have enacted laws to assure the purity of food and the safety of drugs. With the vastly increased use of chemicals since World War II and the greater understanding of the risks they entail to workers, the public, and the environment, the United States and other nations have placed governmental restrictions over the production, sale, use, and disposal of pesticides, industrial chemicals, and chemical wastes. Consumer goods, which may pose chemical or other safety hazards, have also become the subject of regulation in a number of countries.

In recent years, experts have recognized that these national efforts to control hazardous substances often embrace a deadly double standard: Products considered too dangerous or too little studied for use at home are, nonetheless, permitted to be exported freely. This laissez-faire approach reflects the traditional view that each country, as sovereign, has the obligation to protect its own citizens and environment and the right to take action to prohibit or limit imports of hazardous goods. As a result, the prevailing norm in international trade remains *"Caveat Emptor"* or "Let the Buyer Beware."

This is a system primed for abuse. No country alone, even the United States, is able to guard against the mounting tide of potentially dangerous substances moving in international commerce. Yet, as this study has shown, developing nations are the most vulnerable. Simply put, the application of dangerous chemicals has spread throughout the world much more quickly than the capability to assure their safe use. Many developing countries do not have adequate laws or expertise to control hazardous substances. Even where these capabilities exist in poorer nations, they may be underminded by "unholy alliances" between some foreign businessmen and corrupt bureaucrats.[1]

There is no simple remedy to this complex problem. However, in response to growing concern in developing and developed nations, the search for solutions has begun.

### The Quest for a Comprehensive U.S. Policy

In 1977, the U.S. Consumer Product Safety Commission banned the sale of infant pajamas treated with the cancer-causing flame retardant Tris, and ordered their recall from the American market. However, the banned baby garments were not destroyed, and the CPSC initially decided that it lacked the legal authority to halt their export. What followed was the most massive "dumping" to date of a banned product. In just over a year, some 2.4 million Tris-treated garments were rushed overseas. Finally, in May 1978, the CPSC reversed itself under intense public pressure and extended the domestic ban on Tris to cover exports.[2]

The Tris scandal stimulated the start of an intensive examination of U.S. policy on exports of banned products and substances, the first of its kind anywhere in the world. While virtually every substance control statute passed by Congress during the past forty years has addressed the export question, provisions varied widely. At one extreme, prior to 1978, there were no practical restrictions on the sales abroad of banned pesticides or consumer goods or of misbranded or contaminated drugs. At the other extreme, pharmacueticals not approved for sale in the United States cannot be exported at all.[3]

In 1978, both the Carter Administration and Congress began investigations of the hazardous export problem. The administration formed an inter-agency working group, chaired by the President's consumer advisory, Esther Peterson.[4] In Congress, the Committee on Government Operations of the House of Representatives held three days of hearings in July, while both the House and Senate considered closing the export loopholes for banned pesticide and consumer products.

The Congressional initiatives bore fruit first. In October 1978, the House Government Operations Committee issued a *Report on Export of Products Banned by U.S. Regulatory Agencies.*[5] The Committee concluded that:

> The United States has a significant responsibility for the safety of the goods it sells abroad. It cannot condone the export of regulated products which it knows to be harmful either to foreign consumers or the local or world environment . . . . This responsibility must be exercised in a way that respects the sovereignty of other nations and accounts for differing conditions which may affect judgments of health and safety. [6]

Consistent with these conclusions, Congress in late 1978 tightened the export provisions in federal pesticide and consumer product laws. Recognizing that there may be circumstances in which a pesticide or consumer good banned for use in the United States nevertheless may be considered essential or useful elsewhere, Congress did not prohibit exports, but required that foreign governments be provided with notice as to such exports and an opportunity to make their own decisions.[7] Some concerned American organizations have argued that export notices are not sufficient because governments of many importing countries, particularly in the developing world, lack either the technical capability or political will to act upon them. Yet such notices had already resulted in decisions by other countires, including Mexico and South Korea, to halt imports of dangerous substances.[8]

The administration's Interagency Working Group on Hazardous Substances Export Policy remained essentially dormant through 1979. In early 1980, the working group was revived after journalists revealed attempts by American companies to dump toxic wastes in developing countries,[9] and Congressman Michael Barnes introduced a comprehensive and very stringent bill to control hazardous exports.[10]

In August 1980, the inter-agency working group published a proposed U.S. policy for public comment. It was only at this stage that American industry mobilized in opposition to any further tightening of requirements for exports of banned products. Despite extensive behind-the-scenes lobbying by industry, President Carter accepted the recommendation of the working group of January 15, 1981, just five days before leaving office and issued Executive Order 12264, which established a U.S. Hazardous Substances Export Policy. President Carter stated that his policy "emphasizes to other countries . . . that they can trust goods bearing the label 'Made in U.S.A.' "[11]

The executive order had four major components. First, it sought to improve the export notice procedures already required by existing statutes. Second, it called for the annual publication of a summary of U.S. government actions banning or severely restricting substances for domestic use. Third, it directed the State Department and other federal agencies to participate in the development of international hazard alert systems. Fourth, it established procedures whereby formal export licensing controls would be placed upon a very limited number of "extremely hazardous substances" that represented a serious threat to human health or the environment, and the export of which would threaten U.S. foreign policy interests. Export licenses for such substances would be granted only in "exceptional cases" where the importing country, when fully informed, had no objection.

The new policy was met with mixed reviews. Lewis Engman, president of the Pharmaceutical Manufacturers Association, labeled it an "eleventh-hour act of arrogance that would cost American jobs."[12] Many environmental and consumer organizations viewed Carter's order as a step forward, but some complained that it failed to address the problems of relocation of hazardous industries and of products, such as infant formula, which pose special dangers when exported to developing countries.[13]

Thirty-four days later, on February 17, 1981, President Reagan revoked the Carter policy with an executive order entitled "Federal Exports and Excessive Regulation."[14] In testimony at a subsequent hearing on Reagan's action, S. Jacob Scherr of the Natural Resources Defense Council charged:

> With a single sentence, the Reagan administration wiped out two-and-one-half years of study and hard bargaining among more than twenty federal agencies, two sets of Congressional hearings, and the participation of over 100 business, labor, environmental, and consumer organizations here and abroad. The result of this exhaustive review was a finely-honed scalpel which could be used to control exports of only the most dangerous substances, with minimal regulatory burden and impact upon U.S. foreign trade. In contrast, the Regan recission of the [Carter order] reflects a meat-ax approach to federal health, safety, and environmental regulation.[15]

The Departments of State and Commerce were directed by President Reagan to rereview U.S. policy on hazardous exports "to find ways to accomplish the same goals at a lower cost."[16] It soon became clear that the administration and its allies in industry were interested only in undercutting the existing minimal notification requirements for exports of certain banned or regulated substances. In June 1981, the Chemical Manufacturers Association petitioned the Environmental Protection Agency in effect to revoke its export notice regulations for toxic chemicals.[17] In July, the National Agricultural Chemical Association proposed that Congress significantly weaken the export notice provisions in the federal pesticide law.[18]

In September, 1981, a copy of the draft State/Commerce hazardous export review was leaked to the press. Not surprisingly, it recommended that the administration seek to eliminate export notices requirements for toxic chemicals and pesticides. The Commerce Department went even further to urge an end to the U.S. practice of supplying information on federal regulatory actions directly to foreign health and environmental agencies.[19]

Although the Reagan administration appears intent upon abandoning the leadership the United States had taken on this question, the problem of hazardous exports will not go away. Indeed, public concern about trade in hazardous substances has grown substantially. Congressman Barnes has reintroduced his comprehensive bill, and Senator Daniel K. Inouye has submitted legislation specifically aimed at tightening controls on overseas shipments of hazardous wastes.[20] The debate over U.S. policy is likely to continue and intensify in the years to come.

### The Call for International Action

The United States is by no means the only hazardous exporter. Indeed, the nations of Western Europe and Japan, which are major chemical producers, have shown even less sensitivity to the dumping of dangerous products and substances in the Third World. The United Kingdom, France and Switzerland — three major pharmaceutical manufacturing countries — all permit the export of drugs which have not been tested and approved for domestic use.[21] The European Economic Community, which accounts for nearly two thirds of the pesticides in international trade, places no limits on exports of banned or unapproved pesticides, not even the notifications now required in the United States.[22]

Officials of developing countries are beginning to speak out on the issue of dumping and to demand that the industrialized nations recognize their responsibility as exporters of dangerous substances. At the May 1977 meeting of the United Nations Environment Programme (UNEP) Governing Council, Dr. J.C. Kiano, then a Kenyan minister, warned that the developing countries will no longer tolerate seeing their nations used as "dumping grounds for products that have not been adequately tested" and their people used as "guinea pigs" for determining the safety of chemicals. He urged, "Unless a product is fully tested and certified and widely used in the countries of origin, it should not be used for export." He called for the adoption of "international rules and procedures" to halt dumping.[23]

In response to Dr. Kiano's plea, the 58-nation UNEP Governing Council adopted a decision calling for increased cooperation between exporting and importing countries to curb "unethical practices concerning the distribution of chemicals, drugs, cosmetics unfit for human consumption. The decision urged

> governments to take steps to ensure that potentially harmful chemicals, in whatever form or commodity, which are unacceptable for domestic purposes in the exporting country, are not permitted to be exported without the knowlege and consent of appropriate authorities in the importing country."[24]

In 1978, the UNEP Governing Council again discussed the hazardous export problem with a number of developing countries, including Kenya, Bangladesh, Ghana, Iran, Nigeria, and the Philippines, expressing concern; and with a number of industrialized nations, including the United States, Canada, Belgium, and Sweden, agreeing that existing mechanisms for information exchange on chemicals were not effective. The UNEP Governing Council adopted a new decision which reaffirmed its earlier one and also urged that importing countries strengthen their capabilities to make informed decisions as to importation of dangerous chemical products.[25]

In 1979, the United Nations General Assembly addressed the question of hazardous exports for the first time. In a resolution, the General Assembly called upon member states:

> to exchange information on hazardous chemicals and unsafe pharmaceutical products that have been banned in their territories and to discourage, in consultation with importing countries, the exportation of such products to other countries.[26]

This resolution was followed by another in 1980 which asked the U.N. Commission on Transnational Corporations to consider methods for improving information sharing between nations on hazardous exports.[27] It was followed by a third resolution in 1981 which requests U.N. agencies to assist developing countries establish adequate capabilities to guard against imports of banned or severely restricted substances and invites member states to deal with the hazardous export problem through legislation the national level.[28]

These three U.N. General Assembly resolutions provide an outline of new international order for hazardous chemicals. It is based upon all nations recognizing their obligation as sellers of hazardous goods to provide their trading partners with an opportunity for informed consent. However, these resolutions are not binding as a matter of international law, but merely serve as recommendations.

The further development of international standards for trade in banned or severely restricted products is continuing. The Organization for Economic Cooperation and Development (OECD), whose membership consists of 24 western industrialized nations, has already adopted voluntary schemes for sharing information on national actions to ban consumer goods and toxic chemicals. The OECD's Environment and Consumer Policy Committees also have begun discussions on export notification procedures. In Fall 1981, a meeting in Montevideo, Uruguay of senior governmental experts on environmental law identified international trade in hazardous wastes and dangerous chemicals as areas in which UNEP should work towards global treaties.[29]

The United Nations also has become concerned about the role of multinational corporations as hazardous exporters. Multinational corporations can circumvent domestic bans or export restrictions by shifting their production to developing nations or to other less scrupulous exporting countries." Some industry spokesmen have even argued that the problems of "dumping" and abusive marketing practices by chemical companies are illusory. They attempt to blame the dangers of chemicals solely upon misuse, claiming that industry cannot make its product idiot-proof.[30]

There have been efforts within the U.N. system to develop codes of conduct for transnational corporations and the transfer of technology. Both of these codes, which have been under negotiation for a number of years, would require disclosure to the importing country of known health or environmental hazards associated with products or processes to be imported. However, the multinational corporations and the industrialized nations continue to resist the adoption of these codes.[31]

Several of the United Nations agencies, including the World Health Organization, the United Nations Environment Programme, and the International Labor Organization, provide mechanisms for the compilation, assessment, and distribution of data on hazardous chemicals. However, all of these U.N. efforts are voluntary in nature and the essential cooperation of all industrialized countries has not always been forthcoming.

**Citizen Initiatives**

A concerned and organized citizenry is the key to minimizing the dangers posed by hazardous products, processes, and wastes. In the United States and other industrialized nations, environmental and consumer organizatins have long fought for tighter domestic controls on dangerous chemicals and goods. Some of these groups, including the Natural Resources Defense Council (U.S.), Social Audit (U.K.), and the European Environmental Bureau, have more recently focussed upon hazardous exports and advocated an end to the dumping and double standards in international trade. Of equal significance is the establishment of citizen groups in the Third World countries which have sponsored public-education programs and the development of alternatives to the use of dangerous imported chemical products. Just a few examples of these groups are:

The *Consumers' Association of Penang* (Malaysia) is one of the world's largest and most successful grass-roots consumer organizations. CAP works on such issues as nutrition, drug safety and efficacy, and pesticide and industrial pollution. Its purpose is twofold: to warn of hazards, and to teach consumers about their needs and rights of access to product information. CAP's activities include a large library of books and articles about dangerous consumer products; a translation department which receives publications from all over the world; a weekly radio broadcast; a monthly newspaper; seminars and slide presentations; publications; consumer product surveys and tests; and action on consumer complaints.[32]

*APPLE,* the *Association of People for Practical Life Education,* is based in Accra, Ghana. Its approaches to environmental hazards are often innovative, like the campaign to convince Ghanian fishermen to stop poisoning Lake Volta and resume using traps described in Chapter Two.

The *People's Health Center,* Gonoshastrama Kendra (Bangladesh) now brings basic health care to residents of the countryside around Dacca who otherwise would go without. A network of small health care centers, staffed by paramedics, provides preventive care, maternal and child care, family planning, and nutrition advice. People pay, voluntarily, according to their ability. Educational programs are designed to foster self-reliance. For example, the center teaches an inexpensive, safe, and effective treatment for diarrhea — a mixture of molasses, salt, and water, sterilized by boiling. This simple therapy combats dehydration, which kills many infants affected by diarrhea.

The center operates a school, a vocational training program for women, an agricultural cooperative in which all staff take part, and a drug manufacturing plant. Farhad Mazur, marketing director of the drug plant, explains its purpose:

> We want to produce medicine which will. . .[meet] international standards. We'll develop the medicine by ourselves . . .and come up with those medicines essential for our country which the multinational doesn't produce because it is not profitable. At the same time, we'll try to convince our people, our government, that those banned products the multinations are marketing in our country, to stop it.[33]

In addition to producing generic medicines affordable to most people in Bangladesh, the center plans a research and development program to investigate the production of traditional herbal medicines.[34]

Since hazardous exports are a global problem, concerned groups in developed and developing countries have begun to cooperate in exchanging information and developing common strategies. Much of this cooperation is carried out on an ad hoc basis, but the International Organization of Consumer Unions and Health Action International have undertaken to establish formal networks.

The *International Organization of Consumers Unions* head-quartered in The Hague, Netherlands, is a coalition of consumer organizations from fifty countries. It is an independent, nonprofit, nonpolitical foundation whose purpose is to promote worldwide cooperation in consumer protection, information, and education. IOCU has established a "Consumer Interpol" network to exchange international hazardous product warning information, and to promote local, national, and international campaigns against hazardous products. Member organizations promise to publicize the details of known exports or imports of hazardous products and technologies in an effort to force government action.[35]

On May 29, 1981, consumer, professional, development action, and other groups formed a coalition, *Health Action International*, to deal specifically with promotion and sale of pharmaceuticals. The coalition grew out of a three-day conference sponsored by BUKO *(Bundeskongress Entwicklungspolitischer Aktionsgruppen)*, a West German coalition of development action groups. Representatives of non-governmental organizations from twenty-seven countries — half of them developing countries — pledged to resist "the ill-treatment of consumers by multinational drug companies."

Health Action International supports essential drug lists, replacement of proprietary brands by generic drugs, and regional or national production and bulk-buying arrangements. The organization's plans included setting up an international clearinghouse for information on pharmaceutical industry structure, ownership, and marketing practices, and for the coordination of consumer action plans, and working with IOCU's "Consumer Interpol." Withdrawal or restriction of a drug in any one of five "reference" countries (for example, the United States) will trigger immediate communications with the IOCU network.[36]

* * * * * *

The paths to solutions to the problems of international traffic in toxic chemicals, dangerous products, and hazardous wastes, lead in many directions. Although the United States under the Reagan administration is espousing a "free market" philosophy and placing greater reliance upon the private sector and volunteer initiatives, history has shown that industry cannot be relied upon to be self-policing. Nor can citizen groups do the job alone. For so long as the governments of both exporting and importing countries refuse to accept joint responsibility for hazardous commerce, the flow of dangerous substances and defective products in international trade is bound to grow. No single government, international agency, company, or citizen organization has the resources or authority to stem the tide. But each has steps it can take, and to the extent that those are avoided or ignored, all share the burden for the mounting toll of poisoning, of deaths, and of environmental pollution.

# APPENDIX I

# Pesticides and Pills
# FOR EXPORT ONLY

*by*
*Robert Richter*

**Part One: Pesticides**

*Transcript of Television Broadcast*
*on Public Broadcasting Service*
*October 5, 1981*

**NARRATOR:** This film is about double standards, or what some people believe are double standards. It is about certain pesticides and medications we in the United States and other industrial nations export to developing countries in the Third World, products totally banned or severely restricted for only certain uses in our part of the world. Products known to cause cancer and birth deformities in animals, to cause blood disorders, paralysis, blindness, sterility, even death among people.

Why do we find these products unsafe here, but okay for use elsewhere?

**(TITLE)**

In this hour we look at pesticides. In part two, medications.

We filmed in seven different countries in Asia, Africa and Latin America, and found evidence in every one that pesticides banned or restricted here are widely sold, and without restrictions, there.

Some of the largest, most powerful, most profitable corporations in the world have been or are now involved: Mobil, Shell, Dow, Union Carbide, Occidental Petroleum — all from the United States; BASF from West Germany, Imperial Chemical of Britain, Rhone Poulenc of France, and many others.

How it happens, why, who is responsible, what is being done about it, what can be done about it? These are the questions we will address.

**RICHTER:** Here in Washington, DC, I went to the office of the National Agricultural Chemical Association, in the building you see right behind me. They're the trade group that represents the pesticide manufacturers, some of whose products we saw used in different parts of the Third World. This trade association declined to be interviewed.

**NARRATOR:** GIFAP, the organization representing pesticde producers internationally, also refused to be interviewed for this report. Mobil, Dow, Union Carbide and two smaller American firms, declined to be interviewed.

**NARRATOR:** All pesticides used in the United States must be registered with the E.P.A., Environmental Protection Agency. E.P.A. can restrict or prohibit some or all uses, if it finds the risks of using the pesticide outweigh the benefits.

Ironically, we are only just beginning to learn that some banned and restricted pesticides we export are coming back to us as residues on food we import from Third World countries.

**DR. LEE TALBOT:**   An ever increasing use of pesticides in the present way . . .

**NARRATOR:**   Dr. Lee Talbot is former Senior Scientist for the White House Council on Environmental Quality.

**DR. TALBOT** (Director General, International Union for the Conservation of Nature, Switzerland):   Without the use of pesticides diseases like malaria would never have been controlled and would still be a scourge of mankind. Also without the use of pesticides the tremendous increases in agricultural productivity over the past few years simply wouldn't be possible. Without the use of pesticides in the future, the increases in food productivity that are absolutely required for the world's expanding human population would not be possible, will not be possible. So that it's very important to recognize that they represent a major contribution to the welfare of mankind, and indeed to the survival of mankind. But of course, as with any tool there are also problems.

**NARRATOR:**   This is Achedemade Bator, a small village in Ghana, West Africa, about 200 men, women and children, in almost total isolation from the rest of the world. The village is on the shores of Lake Volta. Fish is their main source of protein and their main source of income.

Fishermen from Achedemade Bator showed us how they used to catch fish. They did it by poisoning them with a chemical called Gammalin 20. The fishermen poured it into the lake water, which is also their only source of drinking water. They got the chemical from women who bought small bottles or cans of it in local shops and came to the village to trade for fish.

In the United States, Gammalin 20 is called Lindane. Hooker Chemical, a subsidiary of Occidental Petroleum, produces it. So does Rhone Poulenc of France, Imperial Chemical of Britain, other smaller firms in West Germany and Spain.

Restricting use of Lindane in the United States and Western Europe began in 1969. EPA is currently reviewing additional restrictions because exposure to Lindane may cause cancer and birth deformities in test animals, and because it poisons fish.

The fishermen of Achedemade Bator noticed about a ten percent decline in the number and size of the fish they caught in each of several recent years. Without fish the village cannot survive.

**JOSE LUTZENBERGER** (Environmental leader, Brazil): Here we have some of the products that are used on this farm. Some of them are American, and some are German. Here we have an insecticide, a very potent poison that in '69 killed the fish in 500 kilometers of the

Rhine River in Europe, because a drum fell into the river. Now, when I look at the etiquette here, there is absolutely no reference, first there is no technical name. It's difficult even for a technician, for an agronomist, to find out what it really is, if he doesn't know the makeup. And then there is absolutely no warning to the farmer concerning the danger of the product. In this particular case, the farmer hardly reads Portuguese because he's a Japanese who speaks very little Portuguese. So this gives you an idea of what dangers really these companies are willing to impose on the population.

ANWAR FAZAL:   I have here an insecticide produced by Mobil, which is a corporation from the United States This is manufactured in Holland for them, and sold in Hong Kong and in Malaysia. A test done by our own organization in Hong Kong found that the chemical that is used here, DDVP, exceeds the limits set by the British Safety Standard Scheme. So this would not in fact be allowed for sale in Britain.

NARRATOR: Since Anwar Fazal was filmed Malaysia has banned DDVP. Mobil stopped selling the product in Malaysia but reports that they intend to re-export it.

ANWAR FAZAL: The particular sample in Malaysia doesn't even state what the ingredients are. And here you're dealing with a very large corporation, a very well known corporation, dealing with a product that's very widely used, and you can see the international dimensions.

NARRATOR:   Lake Nakuru, Kenya. There used to be millions of flamingos here. It was a major tourist attraction. Now it is virtually deserted of both birds and tourists. Some believe the decline in the flamingos is due to DDT and Dieldrin found in the waters of Nakuru. E.P.A. banned all crop uses for DDT in 1972 and for Dieldrin in 1974. Most western nations have similar restrictions because DDT causes reproductive failures in birds, and because both DDT and Dieldrin kill fish, cause tumors in animals, build up in the food chain, ultimately into the fatty tissue of people. DDT is produced by Montrose Chemical in America, by other firms in France, Spain and Italy. Dieldrin is made by Shell in Britain.

NAKURU SALES WOMAN (in farm supply store):   DDT twenty-five percent.

NARRATOR:   A farm supply store near Lake Nakuru; pesticides sold without restriction. BHC, banned for all uses by E.P.A. since 1978; Aldrin, a product like Dieldrin, cancelled for all crop uses since 1974; Heptachlor, Chlordane, Endrin, and many other pesticides prohibited or restricted for use in America and many European countries because they have also been found to cause cancer or birth deformities in test animals, or endanger the environment.

Many of these products originate in the United States or Western Europe. Sometimes they are repackaged by local distributors, who also re-label and re-name the products.

At least 200 million pounds a year of pesticides exported from the United States are totally prohibited, severely restricted or never registered for use in our country. Under current United States law this is all perfectly legal.

Exporters of unregistered pesticides must notify EPA they are shipping the product overseas. They also have to notify the importing company. They could be simply notifying their own subsidiary that the pesticide is not registered for use in the United States. It's legal to export unregistered pesticides to any country that will accept them.

**REP. MICHAEL BARNES** (Dem., Maryland): We are in a posture which I find sort of ironic. An Administration that is very pro-business, wants to increase American trade, is actually taking a position that I think is counter to our international trade objectives. If people around the world don't believe that American products are safe, and if we get a reputation around the world for dumping our banned products on other countries, that's not going to help US trade, help American business to sell overseas. I think it's very short-sighted to suggest that the way to promote American business is to sell unsafe products around the world. I just don't think that that's going to prove out.

**NARRATOR:** Malaysia; a rubber plantation.

**MR. LEE** (plantation foreman): When we see an "X" we know that the tree is no longer productive, and therefore it has to be poisoned off. And we have to use 245T because it proves very effective.

**NARRATOR:** 245T — Most uses suspended by EPA since 1979 because it contains a substance called dioxin, one of the most deadly man-made poisons in existence. It causes cancer and birth deformities in test animals at extremely low doses. 245T is part of Agent Orange, the controversial defoliant used during the Vietnam war.

**MR. LEE:** The leaves after being poisoned off, the leaves will drop off, and within a month or so the tree will die. This is very safe. We apply using a brush, and their hands are not in contact with the chemical.

NARRATOR:  Producers of 245T claim the product is safe and have fought all restrictions on its use. Producers include Dow and Union Carbide, headquartered in the United States, and BASF of West Germany.

A small town in Malaysia; a general store. Consumer activist Cha Ket.

CHA KET:  I went into the store to ask whether they sell 245T, and I found that they sell 245T in bottles, and these bottles were kept next to other bottles that contain sauce. They do not have any label. The sauce label has been torn off. We Malaysians do not know much about such products. It has been marketed by multi-national companies for the sake of profit, and they sell it in the rural area which does not know much about such toxic chemicals.

DAVID WEIR (author, *Circle of Poison*, and with Center for Investigative Reporting):  The hypocrisy, the duplicity of saying that what we have found out in this country is too dangerous for us but it's okay to dump it on Third World people, is startling. And furthermore, it seems to me that it is hypocritical in turn to say that we can export our advanced technological products on unsuspecting people, but not export our knowledge and our environmental concerns to those same people.

NARRATOR:  In Bangladesh we learned Dieldrin, Aldrin, Heptachlor and other banned or restricted pesticides are freely sold. Farmers who use these agricultural chemicals don't seem to know what they're using.

QUESTION:  The officials and the irrigation officer, they don't tell you anything?

FARMER (in rural Bangladesh):  No. The day before yesterday one of the officials came. I said, 'Look sir, this plant has a bug and he said take this slip and use this medicine. He didn't explain anything.'

NARRATOR:  Farmers rely on government for reliable information on pesticides. Here's the director of a large government farm in Bangladesh.

QUESTION:  Are there any products you are aware of that are prohibited in the west, US, pesticides, insecticides that are used here?

GOVERNMENT FARM DIRECTOR:  No, we get no such report, that you should not use such and such medicine, such and such pesticide. We don't get any such report from anywhere, even from the producers also.

**QUESTION:** So if a product was banned in the West, would you know about it here?

**GOVERNMENT FARM DIRECTOR:** No, we don't know, we don't know any banned items, whether these are banned by any other producing countries we don't know.

**REP. BARNES:** Well, before any importing country reaches a decision about a product, one of the requirements of our law should be that there is total and complete notification about why the product is banned in the United States, what the health hazards are, what the dangers are to their citizens. That clearly has to be one of the elements of any responsible law, that there be full notification to the potential importer.

**NARRATOR:** A rural Colombia farm supply store.

Mirex, made by Union Carbide, banned by the EPA for all uses in 1977 because it was found to cause cancer in animals, persist in the environent and accumulate in human bodies.

We asked Dr. Julio Mora, the man in charge of pesticides for the Colombia Ministry of Agriculture, why Mirex is sold in his country. Dr. Mora said he never heard of Mirex. He said he didn't know it was cancelled for use in the United States, or that it was sold in Colombia. Nor did he know the United States EPA has issued a list of banned products.

**DR. MORA:** In order for a product to be registered at the Ministry of Agriculture, to authorize its use, it needs the approval of the Health Ministry stating that the product can be utilized. Without such approval it will not be registered. If later on, the product is proven to be very toxic to people's health, we will cancel the product, as long as the cancellation request comes from the Health Ministry.

**DR. ALBERTO GARDEAZABAL** (Colombia Health Ministry): There are many problems because of the frequency in which these pesticides have been coming into our country. The last years have been characterized by a progressive increase in the use of these substances. Also, the government of our country does not have the infrastructure to deal with the rapid importing of so many different pesticides.

**NARRATOR:** Critics charge that exporting companies take unfair advantage of the inability of Third World governments to control and regulate imported pesticides.

**JOSE LUTZENBERGER:** Unfortunately, the multi-national corporations, whether from the U.S. or Europe, are so strong that they managed to transform the Department of Plant Protection in our

Ministry of Agriculture into a true subsidiary of them. Those people take orders from them and carry them out. So we have the case of products that are prohibited in their countries of origin being freely promoted here. Sometimes its not the product that is forbidden in Europe, but certain uses are forbidden there and are fully allowed here.

**NARRATOR:** Many restrictions on pesticide use in western nations are to protect the health of farm workers who apply or are exposed to the chemics. Wherever we filmed in the Third World we saw no protective clothing or masks or any of the other safeguards required in our part of the world.

**QUESTION** (to farm worker in Colombia):    How were you poisoned?

**FARM WORKER:** We stayed here and we were spraying the cotton. One gets poisoned.

**QUESTION:** What happens to a person who is poisoned when spraying?

**FARM WORKER:** They have to run to the doctor. If it is serious they can die.

**NARRATOR:** Alberto Donadio, a Colombia journalist, spoke with another farm worker.

**DONADIO:** Fernando Meneses, you were poisoned two years ago. Tell us what happened to you.

**MENESES:** I was spraying and then at about four I felt sick.

**DONADIO:** What did you feel?

**MENESES:** I felt a burning sensation and then I felt very sick so I left the sprayer there and came home.

**DONADIO:** What were you spraying with?

**MENESES:** Aldrin. They took me to the hospital.

**NARRATOR:** We visited a nearby hospital and spoke to a staff doctor there.

**DOCTOR:** It's been five years that I've been working here in this hospital. During that time I've seen many cases of workers that have come here with pesticide poisoning. Many of the patients have been able to leave the hospital in fairly good condition, but there are others who have died. I think that a profound study should be done to detect the ultimate causes of this problem because pesticide poisoning is one of the main causes for people's need to come to this hospital. I think that the problem has not been studied in depth because there seems to be an interest to hide, or at least minimize, the true magnitude of the problem that we are facing in this area.

**NARRATOR:**   Some people are trying to find out how extensive pesticide poisoning actually is. Dr. Roberto Chediack, a physician working for a group of Central American universities, is doing one survey. Dr. Chediack and his staff have talked to hundreds of workers in coffee plantations, cotton fields and other agricultural areas.

**DR. CHEDIACK:**   Do children help with the harvest?

**WOMAN COFFEE WORKER:**   Yes, they do. That kid carrying stuff over there is my son.

**DR. CHEDIACK:**   The freeness with which they advertise and sell pesticides in Central America has reached a catastrophic level, because it induces a poisoning into the population in general, and to the workers in particular who are the first ones affected within the production process.

Officially in Central America they refer to 5,000 cases of pesticide poisoning, but we believe this is really lower than the actual amount. There have been official meetings that agree with us on this. For example, in Costa Rica they say there are fifteen hundred cases in five years. We looked at a couple of hospitals and found that in three months alone there were 700 cases of poisoning, just in those three months. So in five years there would have been a lot more than they said.

**NARRATOR:**   Cotton is a major crop in which pesticide poisoning among workers has been found, particularly in Latin America. Workers routinely use DDT, Dieldrin, Endrin and other banned or restricted products. When DDT was first used on cotton, it was applied only once or twice a year. But the insects did not all die. Newer and more resistant insects developed, requiring newer and more powerful poisons to kill them. Now cotton is sprayed in some Latin American countries an average of 28 times a growing season.

**LUTZENBERGER:**   What we have is the trans-nationals are promoting products in a way that is totally irresponsible. They have conditioned our farmers to use most of the products even unnecessarily. They have spread the philosophy of preventive use. So you use your poison on a certain day, not because you have a certain pest. Most of the time the farmer doesn't even know what a pest is. He confuses many of his natural predators, of his useful insects, with pests. They have been conditioned to use an insecticide whenever they see anything flying around.

**DAVID WEIR:**   What has happened in the last twenty-five years is that we see succeedingly intensive and over-intensive use of pesticides. Spray planes are taking off every minute in some places in the Third World. They apply them and they over-apply them and abuse them, and pretty soon you have a situation where the pesticide are no longer effective against the pests, and the pests are re-asserting themselves. Insects have tremendous genetic plasticity. They will quickly incorporate an ability to reproduce and to be immune to the effects of the pesticide. So that's what's behind the world-wide resurgence of malaria, where mosquitos that carry malaria no longer can be killed by our common pesticides.

**NARRATOR:**   A banana plantation in Costa Rica.

DDT, Dieldrin and Kepone were used on bananas long after EPA restricted their use, according to US government reports.

Another pesticide that may still be used on these plantations is DBCP. It kills a worm that attacks the banana plant. In 1979 EPA suspended nearly all uses of DBCP because it was found to cause cancer in test animals and to make people sterile.

Castle and Cooke, United Brands and Del Monte insist they stopped using DBCP after it was suspended by the Environmental Protection Agency. Some investigators claim the substance was ex ported from the United States by Amvac Chemical Corporation in 1980, the year after the ban. Amvac refused to tell us if they are currently exporting this chemical.

Whether or not DBCP is used today on bananas is in dispute. But farm workers such as this man, don't know the name or ingredients of the products they do use. The bottle labeled Gramoxone may not have Gramoxone in it. It is simply a convenient container from which he can pour the unknown substance.

Shortly before they are ready to be harvested, workers cover the stalks with pesticide treated plastic envelopes. This worker, like most of those we spoke to, didn't know the name or ingredients of the pesticide. He did know how it affected his health.

**BANANA WORKER:**   The wrapping really bothers me. I have ulcers, and the smell from that bag comes from a powder that they put on it. Around noon when the sun starts getting hot is when it bothers me the most. I get an ache. It is like burning here in the stomach, and it is from the bag. Many of my fellow workers, became poisoned when the liquid, the powder, was being spread around.

**QUESTION:**   What happens if they become poisoned?

**BANANA WORKER:**   They started foaming at the mouth, and then they would have to be taken to the hospital.

**NARRATOR:** A group of workers has petitioned Castle and Cooke to stop heavy spraying. The petition was filed after local studies found workers have low blood counts, dangerously lowering their resistance to disease. Officials at United Brands told us they were not aware of any health problems among banana workers. A Costa Rica union leader working with banana workers, has a different story. Gerardo Delgado.

**GERARDO DELGADO:** Every time that the pesticides are used many people are poisoned. There are even cases of workers who have died due to the use of pesticides. The problem with aerial spraying is that not only are the plantations sprayed, but also the workers who are on the plantations and also the children who come to bring their food. Even at the edge of the plantations at the workers' houses, the substance is also sprayed. So spraying the banana plantation includes spraying the workers, their homes and their families.

**NARRATOR:** We spoke to one banana worker who lives with his family in a small home right next to the plantation.

**BANANA WORKER:** The kids were very sleepy, very sleepy, so we asked the manager to please let us move from the spraying. We thought it was affecting the family. So they moved us and the children stopped being so sleepy. Now the airplanes spray from east to west. The kids come up with all kinds of allergies, irritation of their eyes, and also they get dizzy.

**PROFESSOR GILBERTO CORALES** (Costa Rica University): The problem of the trans-nationals' sale of pesticide products in Costa Rica is an atrocity. I say this because pesticides are used incorrectly. This has serious consequences for our population, for the health of our generation and our children. Our future is being slowly poisoned.

**NARRATOR:** The World Health Organization estimates that 500,000 people suffer from pesticide poisoning every year. At least one percent of these people die from the poisoning. These figures may be low, because they don't take into account miscarriages, birth defects, genetic damage and ecological changes that can affect nutrition. Many cases of poisoning may go unreported. It can also take 15 or more years for some pesticides to inflict their worst damage. And if a worker dies in a rural area of a poor country the cause of death is rarely established.

Ordinary consumers in developing countries who buy and eat certain food also risk health damage from some pesticides. Jose Lutzenberger, environmental leader in Brazil.

**LUTZENBERGER:**   Just recently, we had a tremendous scandal when it was officially recognized that most of our tomatoes were being treated with mercury compounds. And that all our tomatoes on the market were contaminated with mercury. It's well known that mercury is a nerve poison; it attacks the nervous system. In the northern part of the State of Rio de Janeiro, a very high percentage of the workers in the cane fields, where mercury compounds were being used for treatment of the seed, of the cane seed, a very high proportion of the workers were affected, had a very heavy mercury poisoning. And still the product is being used. The big international outfits that produce and sell these products know what's happening. And they know that in the case of tomatoes for instance, where mercury compounds are even against the law, they know that they are selling it where it is being used against the law, and they insist on selling it.

**NARRATOR:**   Another consumer product affected by pesticides is milk. In Central America DDT has been found in cows' milk at a level ninety times greater than the level considered safe in cows' milk in the United States. In milk from nursing mothers, it has been found at levels from six to 200 times higher than the average DDT level in women in the United States.

**NARRATOR:**   Fish are the major source of protein in many Third World countries. This boy is checking a fish trap in rural Bangladesh. Fish are particularly sensitive to pesticides. They feed on poisoned underwater growth, and accumulate the poisons in their bodies. Their ability to reproduce can be damaged. They can die from the poison. Or they can pass it on to people who eat them.

**DR. LEE TALBOT:**   The uncritical use of these pesticides, and particularly the long-lived ones, comes back and negates the gains that the DDT or the other pesticides were initially used to achieve.

**NARRATOR:**   At the village of Achedemade Bator in Ghana the fish catch had declined so much, something had to be done.

A Ghanaian organization taught this villager the connection between the use of Lindane to kill fish, the decline in the fish count, and the effect on the health of the people.

With a flannel board and home made cut-out figures, he explained the situation as he understood it. DDT is the name he uses for any pesticide. He urged the villagers to stop using Lindane.

The fetish priest – witch doctor – was at the meeting. He agreed the practice was dangerous. Later, in a ritual ceremony, he issued a tabu on the use of Lindane.

Other village leaders created a skit. In it, they make fun of the practice of using Lindane to kill fish.

(Skit)

When Lindane poisons people, they actually can get uncontrolled muscle contractions, convulsions, and lapse into a coma. Long term exposure can result in liver damage. Some researchers believe it is linked to blood disorders such as leukemia and aplastic anemia.

The villagers also made up a song in which they ridicule the foolish man who spends money to buy the poisoned fish.

(Song)

At Achedemade Bator, Lindane almost destroyed the village by destroying the productivity of the lake, which is their source of food and livelihood.

In Costa Rica, the productivity of large areas of land have been ruined from pesticide applications. Professor Fernando Morico of the University of Costa Rica.

**PROFESSOR MORICO:**   To complete this tragic picture for Latin America, animals graze on land sprayed with pesticides, and the poison residues are deposited in certain parts of the animals' bodies. The situation reached a critical stage a few months ago when a meat shipment was returned from the United States because it was contaminated with pesticide residues. Also, the problem with this shipment is that the rejected meat that  was returned was eventually sold here by companies that are not Costa Rican.

**DAVID WEIR:**   There are very strong incentives for the Third World countries not to report the true dimensions of their poisoning problems. One of those is, if they say they have a problem with pesticide poisoning, the U.S. and other developed countries are going to monitor their food imports more closely, and therefore they might lose that potential source of foreign exchange. So you actually see a situation where nobody will admit there are any poisonings at all.

**NARRATOR:**   Pesticide producers told us all they are trying to do is help feed a hungry world. Developing nations have critical malnutrition problems, and they need food that pesticide use has made more plentiful.

**DAVID WEIR:**   But our investigation over the years has shown us that at least 50 percent and up to 70 percent of all the pesticides used in Third World countries are not applied to local food products. At least 50 percent and up to 70 are instead applied to export crops, to food that we eat, not people in the Third World eat, to cocoa, to coffee, to bananas, tapioca, all sort of luxury crops, to non-food items like cotton, especially in Central America, to rubber. The application of pesticides in fact bypasses the local need for food around the world.

**NARRATOR:** A coffee plantation in Kenya. Workers live on the plantation right next to the coffee plants. Kenya newspapers have reported that some of their coffee exports have been refused in Europe because of pesticde residues found in and on the coffee beans.

These workers complained to us about skin rashes, headaches and stomach problems as a result of their exposure to pesticides used on the coffee plantations where they work. They don't know the ingredients of the pesticides. All they know is that it hurts them.

The United States Food and Drug Administration has detected DDT, BHC, Lindane, Dieldrin, Heptachlor and other banned or restricted pesticides on coffee beans imported from at least 17 different Third World countries, from Asia, Africa and Latin America. Forty-seven percent of the samples of coffee beans tested by the FDA have been found to be contaminated with these pesticide residues.

**US FDA INSPECTOR** (New York): The lab deals with anything that cannot be seen on the pier itself. The Food and Drug Inspector on the pier looks for things that can be seen. Pesticide residues the lab can find.

**NARRATOR:** Coffee grows within a hard husk, so the pesticide contamination presumably comes up through the roots of the plants into the beans.

Dr. Ian Nisbett, a toxic chemicals expert, is a consultant for EPA and other US government agencies.

**DR. NISBETT:** The pesticides that I have seen reported as turning up as residues in coffee include DDT, Dieldrin, Heptachlor and some of the organo-phosphates. Of those I would think DDT, Dieldrin and Heptachlor would be the most hazardous.

**QUESTION:** And in what sense would they be hazardous? Would they be of concern to consumers in this country who might drink coffee?

**DR. NISBETT:** Those, the three chemicals that I mentioned, DDT, Dieldrin and Heptachlor, all cause cancer in experimental animals, and although most people don't consume very much coffee in the course of a day, it's a matter of concern that we're being exposed to carcinogens in imported food.

**DAVID WEIR:**  The FDA has estimated through spot checks that 10 percent of our imported food is contaminated with illegal residues of banned pesticides. However, the actual amount is much higher. It is actually much higher than that because 70 percent of the known carcinogens cannot be detected by the FDA's analytical methods which check incoming food shipments.

**NARRATOR:**  The bananas that have been sprayed with pesticides from the air, covered with plastic envelopes coated with other pesticides, that have grown from land soaked with still other pesticides, are now getting ready to be shipped overseas. They sprayed one last time before the company labels are stuck to each bunch.

**DR. NISBETT:**  I know that a lot of pesticides are used on bananas, specifically DDT, Dieldrin and Kepone have all been used in very large quantities on bananas in Central America. Of those the only one I know of in which residues have been found in bananas brought into the United States, is DDT. But I would assume that there are the residues of the other chemicals.

**QUESTION:**  What would that mean in terms of human health here in the United States, to have those residues found on bananas?

**DR. NISBETT:**  That would depend on the quantities, I think. And I'm not aware of extensive studies of how much DDT and Dieldrin is found on bananas. The fact that it's used in large quantities would give one ground for concern.

**DAVID WEIR:**  In Central America the pesticides are applied to the fields which grow coffee, bananas, cocoa, rubber, cotton, non-food products. All of these things are then shipped back to the United States, which completes the circle of poison in a sort of final irony, the boomerang effect, where we have our foods and our goods contaminated with residues of banned pesticides. And the ships come right back here, and the stuff proceeds to market.

**NARRATOR:**  The circle of poison from the double standard of exporting pesticides found unsafe here, leaves a trail of victims throughout the world, from workers who handle it, to farm laborers exposed to it, families who live near the farms and plantations, consumers overseas and here in our own country. When it reaches home we start paying attention. Can the circle ever be broken?

**REP. BARNES:** Right at the very end of the Carter Administration, the President issued an Executive Order which didn't go as far as I would have liked, but it went a long way toward regulating the export of hazardous products. When President Reagan came into office he immediately rescinded that Executive Order. Shortly after that we held hearings in Congress to find out what the new administration's posture was going to be. They refused to send a witness up. So there has been sort of a see-saw on the question over the past couple of years.

**DR. LEE TALBOT:** The international community is taking what actions it can. In our view these are entirely inadequate so far. And unless this problem is licked, there is simply no way we can lick the problem of the misuse of pesticides with its consequent damage to human welfare, and indeed human survival.

**ANWAR FAZAL:** Greed is a very very important aspect of this whole problem, and changes are going to come slowly. They're also going to come only if we have more and more citizen groups throughout the world alert about these kinds of problems.

**JOSE LUTZENBERGER:** Personally we are fighting as best we can against this scandal. But since on our side we have only a very reduced number of people who are all idealists fighting in their free time, and with their own means, and without any help . . . On the other hand we have armies of well paid technicians, many of them paid in foreign currencies, so it really is a tremendous fight still that we have. So what we need is more consciousness, more people fighting.

**NARRATOR:** Raising consciousness among the villagers of Achedeemade Bator led to action that saved the fish and saved the village. In 1979 they stopped using Lindane to catch fish. Now they use nets and traps, and the fish are again becoming plentiful.

But Achedemade Bator is only the first village in Ghana to stop using poison to kill fish. Consciousness raising and education on safe pesticides is a worldwide health issue, and has a long way to go in Ghana, and everywhere else.

Organizing groups to fight for responsible change is only starting. Legislators are only just beginning to press for new laws. International organizations have passed resolutions only now beginning to be implemented. Resistance by governments and corporations remain huge barriers to be overcome.

As Third World people become more aware of the problem, resentment and anger grows. It will continue to grow until we all find some way for the circle of poison to be broken.

**ANNOUNCER:** The issues examined in this documentary are complex. Although the Pesticide Industry declined to participate in this program, GIFAP, their international representative, expressed the industry position in correspondence with the producer:

Pesticides are essential for modern agriculture.

Each government is competent and responsible for determining its own policies on the export and import of pesticides.

The Reagan Administration is reviewing U.S. export policies for hazardous exports. It is reported to favor eliminating rules which require pesticide manufacturers to notify foreign governments before exporting goods found too dangerous for general use in the U.S.

## CREDITS

*Produced by*
ROBERT RICHTER

*Writer/Reporter*
ROBERT RICHTER

*Associate Producer*
JACQUELINE LEOPOLD

*Cinematography*
BURLEIGH WARTES

*Editor*
PETER KINOY

*Additional Editing*
MOLLY SMOLLETT

*Assistant Editor*
ANNE SAHL

*Sound:*
*Latin America*
PAMELA YATES

*Asia, Africa*
SAMANTHA HEILWEIL

*United States*
GILL McDOWELL
CHERYL GROFF

*Europe*
VLADIMIR HAVEL

*Research*
VINCENT COLUCCIO
JACQUELINE LEOPOLD

*Production Secretary*
SALLY GROO

*Production Liaison*
*Malaysia*
EDMUND GNANAMUTHU

*Bangladesh*
FARHAD MAZHAR

*Kenya*
CARY AYUB

*Ghana*
ROBERT RUSSELL

*Brazil*
TONY BERARDI

*Colombia*
GERARDO REYES

*Special thanks*

Association of People for Practical Life Education, Ghama, DR. MARIAN MOSES, LUIS ARGUETA/DAVID TEMPLE

For WNET — *Coordinating Producer,* KATHY KLINE; *Executive Producer,* DAVID LOXTON

*This program was made possible by a grant from:* INDEPENDENT DOCUMENTARY FUND, which is supported by NATIONAL ENDOWMENT FOR THE ARTS, FORD FOUNDATION and CORPORATION FOR PUBLIC BROADCASTING

*Additional funding provided by:* FILM FUND, BYDALE FOUNDATION, CS FUND, SAMUEL RUBIN FOUNDATION, UNITED NATIONS ENVIRONMENTAL PROGRAM, DANCHURCH AID, MAILMAN FOUNDATION, METHODIST BOARD OF GLOBAL MINISTRIES, OXFAM, ROCKEFELLER FAMILY ASSOCIATES, NEW LAND FOUNDATION

*and:* STEVE ALLEN, MRS. GARDNER COX, ROBERT BOYAR, CANADIAN LABOR CONGRESS, DR. MAX DELBRUCK, PAULINE STAHL SCOTT, KEN WYMAN, ACAO DEMOCRATICA FEMININA GNOCHA

*A production of* ROBERT RICHTER and the Television Laboratory at WNET/THIRTEEN

# Pesticides and Pills
# FOR EXPORT ONLY

*by*
*Robert Richter*

## Part Two: Pharmaceuticals

*Transcript of Television Broadcast*
*on Public Broadcasting Service*
*October 7, 1981*

**NARRATOR:** This film is about double standards, or what some people believe are double standards. It is about certain pesticides and medications we in the United States and other industrial nations export to developing countries in the Third World – products totally banned or severely restricted for only certain uses in our part of the world. Products known to cause cancer and birth deformities in animals, to cause blood disorders, paralysis, blindness, sterility, even death among people. Why do we find these products unsafe here, but okay for use elsewhere?

**(TITLE)**

In this hour we look at medications.

We filmed in seven countries in Asia, Africa and Latin America. The practice goes on everywhere we went. Some of the largest pharmaceutical companies in the world are involved: Ciba Geigy and Hoffman LaRoche from Switzerland; Hoechst from West Germany; Glaxo from Britain; Upjohn, Pfizer, Sterling, Foremost McKesson and Squibb — all headquartered in the United States; and many other smaller firms in Europe and Japan.

Third World people buy close to three billion dollars worth of medicine every year, imported from our part of the world.

This young Japanese woman is blind and paralyzed, and in constant severe pain. It happened after she took a drug made from clioquinol. Clioquinol is marketed by Ciba Geigy as a cure for common or severe diarrhea. Ciba is a large, Swiss-based international drug and pesticide company, with factories in 76 countries, including the United States. One of the many brand names Ciba sells clioquinol under is Enterovioform.

There are over 10,000 people in Japan who are suffering from SMON, the short-hand name for the destruction of the nervous system caused by clioquinol products.

Ciba has taken these products off the market in Japan and the United States since the early 1970s. What about the availability of clioquinol products in the rest of the world?

**RICHTER** (in Malaysia drug store): Enterovioform? Ciba Geigy? Here you are (pays for product).

**RICHTER** (In Nairobi, Kenya): I was just in the pharmacy that you see behind me, and although I was told you normally need a prescription, I was able to walk in and buy Enterovioform under another name. It's called Mexase. It's made by Ciba Geigy, the same manufacturer that makes Enterovioform. This is Enterovioform plus an enzyme.

**NARRATOR:** We bought clioquinol products in Asia, Africa and Latin America. All were made by Ciba Geigy and sold under various brand names — Enterovioform, Mexase and Mexaform, among others. Different brands in each country had different information about indications — that is, what the product should be used for; and contra-indications — that is, when it should not be used, as well as different information about side effects and warnings. Some had no information at all. We went to Basel, Switzerland, Ciba's international headquarters, to ask them about what appears to be a significant inconsistency.

**DR. WALTER VON WARTBURG** (Pharmaceutical Policy, Ciba Geigy): I would assume that we have a pretty consistent policy with regard to information contained in the package leaflet, and that we try to enforce this policy throughout the world.

NARRATOR: Arturo Lomelli, Director, Mexico Consumers Union.

ARTURO LOMELLI: Ciba laboratory, which manufactures Enterovioform, sells it under thirteen different brand names. This shows us the lack of ethics on the part of this lab, to provide thirteen different sets of instructions for the same product, under the assumption that there are basic differences in people, when there is only one mankind. In our country the situation is even worse because with one there are no instructions whatsoever. We call this the fourteenth set of instructions, the non-existent one. On this fourteenth package there are no indications regarding its purpose, the limitations of its use and the side effects that it may cause, or what the dosage should be. It is sold like candy. And we know it is a medicine that has already caused injury and death to thousands of people in Japan.

NARRATOR: Japanese clioquinol victims and their families took to the streets, perhaps the first organized public demnstration ever against a medical product. The health problems from clioquinol came to light in Japan because of that country's sophisticated medical system and equipment that can measure trace amounts of chemicals in the body. The victims successfully pressured Ciba and its Japanese subsidiary to stop selling the product. The Japanese court ordered Ciba to pay millions of dollars to over 4,000 clioquinol-damaged people.

DR. VON WARTBURG (Ciba Geigy): We felt that being constantly in the court of public opinion while fighting the case, would in the end do much more damage to the company than to show a certain faith or compassion by saying there are victims right now. There is a big likelihood that our drugs are involved. Therefore, let's compensate the victims now and let's not compensate the sons of the sons of the victims twenty years from now, if at that time a court has come to a conclusion that we are really libel.

NARRATOR: The leading international spokesman for the pharmaceutical industry is Michael Peretz.

MR. PERETZ (Executive Director, International Federation of Pharmaceutical Manufacturers Associations):I don't want to defend clioquinol specifically, but could I say at least there is some doubt as to whether the SMON was the result of using clioquinol in the recommended doses. If indeed it's true that the Japanese, because of their particular conditions, tend to swallow clioquinol by the handful, then it isn't necessarily abusing the drug, or it isn't necessarily to ban the drug in other countries where it is being used under proper recommended dose conditions. And that is what some authorities appear to believe.

**NARRATOR:** No reliable data has yet been developed about clioquinol victims in Third World countries. But medical experts have identified over 100 victims in Europe, including this woman in Sweden, who is losing her ability to walk and see.

**SWEDISH WOMAN:** At the suggestion of the doctor, I went down to the Canary Islands. At that time I did not know that the drug Enterovioform was dangerous. Before leaving for the islands I asked the doctor what to take to protect myself from the various stomach viruses one could contract in traveling to the Mediterranean countries. I was told by several doctors that Enterovioform was the only drug to take.

**MAN'S VOICE:** How well can you see now?

**SWEDISH WOMAN:** Sometimes it is totally light, sometimes gray, sometimes dark or completely black. I cannot read or see the TV picture any more.

**CIBA GEIGY OFFICIAL:** We believe as a consolidated kind of medical opinion in house, that these drugs nevertheless are very valuable if properly used, and we continue to sell them in the industrialized countries and in the Third World as well, because we clearly see that there is a need for these drugs, in view of the fact that alternative treatments are not easily available.

**NARRATOR:** Medication may be appropriate for some kinds of diarrhea, but there are alternative ways to combat most common forms of this disease. In this clinic in Bangladesh the local population is learning how to cope with diarrhea by using a simple home remedy, instead of medical products from western nations that may be hazardous. The World Health Organization, WHO, has estimated that one child out of ten in the Third World dies before they reach the age of five, because of diarrhea-related health damage. The paramedic stresses the importance of continuing to give food and liquids to children with diarrhea. She also suggests giving children a mixture of molasses, salt and boiled water. It will probably relieve the symptoms for most children.

Anwar Fazal, Director, International Organization of Consumers Unions.

**ANWAR FAZAL:** There is in the current world today a great deal of behavior by corporations that is unconscionable. And there is no reason for this kind of violence that's being committed to Third

World consumers, to consumers even in developed countries. There's also no reason for the kind of marketing strategies that are being used, the kind of mis-information, the kind of lack of information that is being provided to consumers of the world.

**NARRATOR:** Dr. Milton Silverman, a University of California pharmacologist and author of *Prescription for Death.*

**DR. SILVERMAN:** I think it's most important to bear in mind that the pharmaceutical industry has done far more good than it has done harm. It has brought out products . . . this is the world drug industry, but the United States in particular, brought out products that have wiped out many once fearsome plagues of the past. It has reduced crippling, suffering, made recovery quicker and more certain. But it is not perfect; and the practices that I have been worrying about, and many other people have been worrying about, is no trifling problem. It concerns hundreds of thousands of people a year in the Third World, and it is a blemish on an industry which is now grossing sales in the tens of billions of dollars a year.

**NARRATOR:** There are two kinds of medicines we focused on . . . The kind severely restricted for use in western nations, and the kind that are totally banned, or have been taken off the market in our part of the world because they've been found to be unsafe.

**WOMAN AT NAIROBI SHOW** (Selling "Bronchominit" in Swahili)

**RICHTER** (in Nairobi): At the Nairobi International show they're advertising this product at the Glaxo pavilion, a British pharmaceutical firm exhibit. It happens to be a cough syrup that they say should be used for babies. And the first ingredient listed is chloroform. Chloroform products are banned in the West — in the U.S., Canada and other nations — because they've been found to cause liver and heart damage in people.

**MICHAEL PERETZ** (Executive Director, IFPMA): The chloroform and peppermint are in there strictly as keeping agents and flavoring agents. They're not in there for any therapeutic reason whatsoever.

**NARRATOR:** Dr. Martin Khor, Research Director for the Consumers Association of Penang, Malaysia.

**MARTIN KHOR:** Chloroform is sold in Malaysia. It is found in six cough mixtures at least, in our survey, and two brands of toothpaste, including the very popular MacLeans.

NARRATOR: Here's another banned medicine sold without restriction in the Third World.

RICHTER (on camera, in Costa Rica and Kenya): Albamycin-T, a combination antibiotic, prohibited in the United States, manufactured by Upjohn. It's a product formerly known as Panalba, and it's been banned in the United States for over ten years because one in five patients who took it had an allergic reaction to it.

DR. BRUNO CUNHA (Dept. of Pharmacology, University of Sao Paolo, Brazil): This is a product that has been taken out of the American market for over ten years. But it sells in Brazil, and rather freely. If we go over to the Brazilian manual and try to look up about Albamycin we'll see the information is very very short. It just gives the name of the antibiotic and says that it is used for urinary infections, and it doesn't say anything, absolutely nothing on the toxicity or side effects. So, if a physician tries to get some information about the product, or he is about to prescribe for the patient, he doesn't get anything from here. He thinks that it's just a normal antibiotic, made by an American company, probably approved for use in the United States, and should be used here.

DR. MILTON SILVERMAN: In the United States most physicians have been trained to use what we call . . . it's official name is "PDR," the *Physician's Desk Reference*. It's very often called the "Prescriber's Bible." It contains descriptions of the most important prescription drugs that are used in the United States, and these descriptions are the ones approved by the Food and Drug Administration. They give a complete disclosure of both the good things and bad things about each of these drugs.

In Latin America the comparable books, which are not approved by the government, have outrageously exaggereated descriptions of the drugs. They make claims which cannot be supported by scientific fact. This is true for most of the countries in Africa and in Asia. And so far as dangers are concerned, these are glossed over, or totally ignored.

NARRATOR: Pregnant women, nursing mothers and children are especially susceptible to dangerous side effects from certain severely restricted medicines that the American *Physicians Desk Reference* warns doctors about in our country. In the Third World when the packages don't have these warnings, and are without restrictions on who can buy them, taking these products can lead to serious health problems.

We sent our sound recordist into this drug store in Nairobi, Kenya, and for a 3 year old girl she said wasn't eating well she was able to get Dianabol, an anabolic steroid.

**RICHTER** (in Nairobi): The druggists said it was simply Vitamin C with a hormone added. It happens to be something that is used in the States on prescription for a bone disorder and is known to cause the stunting of growth of little boys, and to cause permanent sex changes in little girls.

**RICHTER** (in Colombia): Here is Dianabol, the anabolic steroid that is sold as an appetite stimulant for children, as this insert from a Dianabol package specifically suggests.

**RICHTER** (in Zurich, interviewing Martin Peretz): Are anabolic steroids for example, something that should be given to a child as an appetite stimulant?

**MR. PERETZ:** No, not at all.

**RICHTER** (in Basel, inteviewing Dr. Von Wartburg): In Asia, Africa and Latin America we bought a product called Dianabol, manufactured by Ciba Geigy. In the United States it says that this product can cause irreversible sex changes in children. Nothing about that is stated in these packages or in any of the information that is in comparable publications supplied to physicians in Asia, Africa and Latin America. Why?

**DR. VON WARTBURG:** If this is the case, it's not a question of policy, it is a question of lack of implementation of that policy. The blame can either be on our side − if this is the case I would very much deplore it − but it can also be on the side of the authorities in the respective countries, that they have not yet given permission to the changes, that bureaucratic elements were involved, or any kind of other impediments which have led to that situation.

**RICHTER:** Why don't you just take Dianabol off the market until you're able to supply the correct information to the consumers?

**MR. VON WARTBURG:** Because this would be a complete over-reaction. Because if we have the medical kind of evidence that this problem may arise, what we have to do is first to inform the authorities.

**RICHTER:** A child could be taking this product right now who shouldn't be taking it, who will suffer the damages because you are acting too slowly. Can you not act more quickly?

**MR. VON WARTBURG:** This is always a question on what means would best serve a certain end. If we were starting to send out letters every day on every new case of a changing indication, a new warning statement, we would probably swamp the world that much with all kinds of new medical evidence that in the end nobody would read it.

**NARRATOR:** Ciba revised the package insert for Dianabol in May of 1981.

**MR. VON WARTBURG:** As of now the text which ought to be in the package leaflets on a worldwide scale should include the warning statement with respect to virilization, along the lines of the F.D.A.

**NARRATOR:** This is the FDA approved information on Dianabol in the American *Physicians Desk Reference*. It states Dianabol is probably effective in treating bone degeneration in old people and is without value as primary therapy. Under Adverse Reactions, a number of sex changes are listed for males who take Dianabol, and many "irreversible sex changes" among females. There is an even longer list of severe Adverse Reactions for both males and females who take Dianabol.

The May 1981 Dianabol package insert still claims the product is useful for appetite stimulation, and lists eight indications, that is, conditions when the product could be used, compared to only one indication permitted in the U.S. And under "Unwanted Effects" the latest package insert lists only one irreversible sex change for females, compared to the long list that has been in the American reference manual since 1973.

**RICHTER** (in Zurich, interviewing Mr. Peretz): If you have a warning about a product in the United States or westrn Europe that if you take this product it can cause permanent sex changes in a child, and this information is not given about that same product by the same manufacturer in a Third World country, what would you say about that?

**PERETZ:** Very reprehensible.

**NARRATOR:** This is how the African version of the American Physician's Desk Reference describes Dianabol. They state it is for "promotion of growth in underdeveloped children" and no adverse effects at all are noted. In the Asian manual for doctors Dianabol is called Dianavit, with doses listed for children; no adverse reactions listed. In the Mexican Physicians Desk Reference, Dianavit is described in more detail, also with doses for children listed, but nothing about sex changes that are irreversible.

But Dianabol or Dianavit are not the only anabolic steroids sold freely in the Third World.

**DR. RAYMUNDO ORDONEZ** (Mexico City, physician): Winstrol, prohibited in the United States for children. Here they sell it freely as a tonic.

**RICHTER** (in Malaysia drug store): This is Winstrol, which it says is sold for weight loss, anorexia, in case you don't eat.

**RICHTER:** And it comes from the U.S.?

**WOMAN PHARAMCIST:** Yes.

**RICHTER:** Winthrop

**WOMAN PHARMACIST:** U.S.A.

**RICHTER** (in Sao Paulo): Here , we bought, for example, Winstrol, this time as an injectible product.

**NARRATOR:** The American *Physicians Desk Reference* states Winstrol should only be used for adults for a blood disorder. Contra-indications are listed in detail, precautions in detail; a listing of sex changes, "usually irreversible" even after prompt discontinuance of taking the product.

Here is the description in the Brazilian medical manual. The information comes from the same manufacturer. These twelve lines are all the facts on Winstrol this manual contains. No problems noted.

Here is Winstrol described in the African directory most commonly used by physicians on that continent. The information again comes from the same manufacturer.

**RICHTER** (in New York): Winstrol products are made by Winthrop Sterling, a subsidiary of Sterling Drug Company. They're head-quartered in the building right behind me in New York. We asked to film an interview with anybody from Sterling Drug about why they market Winstrol the way they do in Third World. They refused to be interviewed.

**QUESTION:** In America, product 'X' is supplied with certain information by the manufacturer. The same manufacturer supplies different information in a Third World country. Why?

**MR. PERETZ:** Because there may be no doctors there to understand what the relevance of the particular medical terms. You have to look at the whole medical infrastructure before you can answer this question.

**NARRATOR:** In the developing world the medical infrastructure is often inadeqate. When someone becomes ill they rarely can afford to go to a doctor for help. And few doctors are available, especially in rural areas. In the United States there is one doctor for every 500 people; in Bangladesh, one for every 90,000.

Getting medicine is easy however, if you can afford it. Rules permitting sale of certain medicine by prescription only, rigorously followed in the United States and western Europe, are ignored or nonexistent in most Third World countries. In Malaysia, Martin Khor has been gathering evidence about these products, sold without restriction, in his country.

**DR. MARTIN KHOR:** Another drug is Phenacatin, which causes kidney failure, which is often fatal. It is sold here under the brand name of Saridon, which is sold by the Swiss multi-national, Roche, and as we can see from this advertisement, it is being recommended for all sorts of minor ailments, such as toothaches, flu headaches, and so on. Another drug which is sold, another brand of phenacatin, is Dusil. Now this has been very widely advertised in our television and in our films. When I was a schoolboy I remember it being advertised as "Dusil makes life worth living again," if you have any headache or if you have stomach aches. And it's being widely advertised still today in Malaysia. "When in pain or depressed, take Dusil." It gives the impression that it even cures you from your emotional problems.

**NARRATOR:** Among the most heavily advertised products in many developing countries are so-called vitamin tonics. Many contain up to 30% alcohol. Consumers rarely know the potential hazards of such products. Head of the People's Health Center in Bangladesh, Dr. Zafroullah Chowdhury.

**DR. ZAFROULLA CHOWDHURY:** This is a drug made by Squibb. This is a U.S. multinational company. If you open it, no literature inside. You can check it. Nowhere mentioned a contra-indication. Look at it, no contra-indication, no contra-indication, no contra-indication mentioned. On the contrary, what they're promoting is giving vitality, energy. Verdiviton is allowed in Britain for a limited use, where it has been categorically mentioned anybody having a problem with liver, this drug not to be used. Country like Bangladesh, more than fifty to sixty percent of the people suffer from either amoebic hepatitis or some other ailments of the liver. In other words, this drug is contra-indicated for the population of Bangladesh.

NARRATOR: When people get sick in the Third World most of them go to a pharmacist for medical advice and drugs, instead of seeing a doctor. So precise information about medical products is critical for pharmacists. Head of the Pharmacists Association of Brazil, Pedro Zidoi.

PEDRO ZIDOI: There is a problem with products licensed for sale in the country of origin, for example the United States. When the product is sold in Brazil many of the restrictions that exist in the United States don't accompany the registration of the product in Brazil. The multinational companies aim the information more toward doctors and they don't seem to have any interest in the pharmacies.

PHARMACIST IN DACCA, BANGLADESH: When the doctor prescribes, the patient comes to us, submits the prescription. Then we sell it to him. The adverse effects, the contra -indications should be known to the doctor better than us. Isn't that it?

NARRATOR: How do Third World doctors actually learn about pharmaceutical products?

DR. ZAFROULLAH CHOWDHURY: The multinationals, they have got even on hot summer days, they put their detail men, their representative, with the posh clothes, the neckties, suit and other. These are the people who are providing the information to the doctors. When he goes he says this is a wonderful drug. New drug has come. And doctor has got in this country no other information source.

DR. KODAWALALLA (Nairobi, Kenya): A poor doctor has to go by what is advertised to him, what is recommended to him, has to go by what is available in the country. And he has no means of checking up all the things. He would prescribe what he thinks is right.

DR. SILVERMAN: We would hope that a company would tell the truth, all the truth about its products. Particularly to keep physi-because they took the drug, you are only saying people who are suffering the side effects. You can create your own philosophy to justify it. But when you compare two packages, one in America and one in Brazil, you cannot avoid the feeling that a crime is being committed.

NARRATOR: One of the many brand names for Dipyrone is Bonpyrin.

**MARTIN KHOR** (Malaysia): This is very popular in Malaysia. It is very widely sold. And according to one doctor whom we interviewed, "This drug," I quote from him, "should be banned from the face of this earth," because he himself has personally seen two children die from shock after taking this drug.

**DR. SILVERMAN:** I was interested and rather horrified to be told by representatives of some of the European drug companies that market these substances, that "Isn't it fortunate that they don't produce any damage in the Third World? There's something in the tropics or whatever it is, that protects patients from getting this horrible blood destruction." Actually, it doesn't tell you anything of the kind. In those countries there either are not enough facilities or money or manpower to make blood tests. Nobody knows what the white count is.

**ARTURO LOMELLI** (Mexico): In Mexico there are more than ninety brands that contain dipyrone, but none of them say anything about indications, what the product should be used for.

**RICHTER** (in Nairobi): Here we are in Nairobi, Kenya; and in this pharmacy just behind me I was able to walk in and come out with Novalgin, also made with Dipyrone. This is made by Hoechst, a German pharmaceutical company.

**NARRATOR:** Novalgin is also widely used in Bangladesh. The economic power of multinational companies like Hoechst can make it difficult for a Third World government to stop selling potentially hazardous drugs like Novalgin, or "Novalzin" as Dr. Chowdhury calls it.

**DR. CHOWDHURY:** The government of a Third World country like Bangladesh, is in a very difficult situation. They tried to stop Novalzin. It is banned in the USA. But it is going on; the government for the last four years they couldn't stop it. They say it will continue until 1981. Who knows. There will be a change of government and through some manipulation, some maneuvers, this drug with a different name, will continue to flourish in the market.

**DR. M.A. MATIN** (Minister of Health, Bangladesh): They are producing in this country some Novalgin tablets, but we will review it again in the month of December, when our Drug Technical Advisory Board will take a final decision on it. Because the hazards which have been said, we do not get such type of results in our patients and clients. So it is doubtful whether it is harmful.

**NARRATOR:** Dr. Chowdhury's prediction was accurate. The Bangladesh government has postponed until 1983 any decisions on Novalgin.

**DR. VON WARTBURG:** The decision on whether a drug can be marketed, and with what kind of software it can be marketed — software being the accompanying literature — is in all countries of the world a decision taken by the government representatives, say the Public Health Authority.

**BERNARDO KUCINSKI:** The behavior of the Health Authority has been the typical behavior of someone who is involved with the misbehavior. And I wanted to give you one example, for instance. I have been writing about this subject in Brazil for years, and I can show you articles I have written about drugs, about this kind of subject, being censored by the police, the Federal Police, in the newspaper I was working at that time. In countries like Brazil, in Third World countries, big government and transnational companies are very much promiscuous. I mean you have a Minister of State; today he's a minister, tomorrow he's president of a transnational company. Today the fellow is the General of such and such army. Tomorrow he's vice president of a transnational company.

**DR. SILVERMAN:** A lot of us think these companies are actually getting away with murder. And we wonder why somebody hasn't stopped it. There are people within the governments, within the ministries of health in these countries, who wonder the same thing. Many of these government officials would like to have real tough laws on their books which they could enforce. But it's difficult if not impossible to get the parliament or the legislature to pass such legislation. And even if the laws are passed, it is difficult if not impossible to put teeth into it. There is unquestionably bribery of either government officials or physicians themselves by the industry. This is an accepted fact of life, actually an accepted fact of life and death in the Third World.

**DR. JOHN JENNINGS** (Vice President, Science, U.S. Pharmaceutical Manufacturers Association): Certainly all of the information relating to the efficacy and the hazards of drugs produced in this country is available to the regulatory authorities of other countries. The problem I think is with people. We have problems with people all over the world. I think there are deficiencies and defects, and occasionally even abuses.

NARRATOR: Some Third World governments have deliberately chosen to use certain restricted drugs because they claim they are essential for the exceptional needs of their nation — to help with such problems as overpopulation. One such drug is Depo-Provera, a hormone produced by Upjohn, an American firm. It is used by millions of women in many Third World countries, including here in Bangladesh. Depo-Provera is promoted for birth control at this family planning rally. The Minister of Health calls for everyone to go along with family planning, including the use of Depo-Provera. The drug is not approved for birth control use in the United States.

DR. MATIN (Minister of Health, Bangladesh): So in view of our pressing problem of population, and in view of the fact that this is so easy to administer in the rural areas, and in view of the fact that our people like it so much, and in view of the fact that there is no definite evidence that it causes harm to the human being, we have decided to sort of use it in centers where there are medical facilities and where there is a system of supervision.

NARRATOR: One injection of Depo-Provera is powerful enough to prevent conception for thirteen weeks. Most Third World women who are injected don't know Depo-Provera is not approved for birth control in the United States. It is suspected of causing cancer in test animals, and has been linked to many reproductive irregularities. Critics claim that some injected women who later wanted children were infertile.

DOCTOR L. J. RASUL (talks with Bangladesh woman who has just been injected with Depo-Provera): Her husband really doesn't want it, but she would rather have another son later on.

NARRATOR: In New York, the Population Council has been study-ing the use of Depo-Provera around the world. Senior Researcher Dr. Bruce Scherer.

DR. SCHERER: It isn't clear from the current data whether Depo-Provera causes cancer in animals. And it isn't clear, indeed, if it did, what that would mean for humans. But the fact that in two ex-periments, in two species of animals in which these studies have been done, there have ben indications of problems, suggests to me this is a drug we need to look very closely at, before going to full distribution on a global scale with it.

DR. RASUL: This injectible contraceptive is good for our country, the ladies in our country, because it is very convenient. It doesn't cause much health hazards, like cancers and all, because people die more of giving birth to children than of cancer in our country.

**DR. SCHERER:** I think it's important to ask the question "Is the method less safe, as safe, or safer than the alternative, namely having an unwanted pregnancy?" But I think it's also important to ask "Is the method safe at all? What is the method going to do to me? How convenient is it, how effective is it, how pleasant is it to use, what are its long term hazards, if any?" These aren't questions that can be brushed aside by a risk-benefit assessment that only focuses on the issue of pregnancy.

**DR. RASUL:** It is a valuable method, yes, just to control the birth rate, but as a hormone it has got some hazards.

**ANWAR FAZAL:** The basic principle should be that there should be no discrimination, no double, treble, or quadruple standards. There can be exceptional circumsatnces. And it is important for us to recognize that. I think a number of countries would want these circumstances to be recognized. But we're concerned that people hide behind these exceptional circumstances, and make that the rule, to do what they want to do wherever they want to do it. And that we are not prepared to accept.

**BERNARDO KUCINSKI:** I would say that the starting point of changing of the situation in Brazil would be to copy the rules of the FDA, to take all of the rules of the FDA and to copy them, and to translate them into Portugese, and to force the companies to obey the same proceedings.

**DR. BRUNO CUNHA** (Brazil): First, on the side of the companies, they really should establish a mono-ethical standard. I think this could be done even by interference of World Health Organization. It could establish that companies have to work with the same ethical standards in any country.

**DR. JOHN JENNINGS** (Science Vice President, Pharmaceutical Manufacturers Association, U.S.): We do subscribe to the idea that prescribing information for particular drugs should be essentially the same throughout the world. This is embodied in both the PMA code and the IFPMA code.

**DR. VON WARTBURG:** I would propose that any one body, be it the FDA, your Food and Drug organization, be it the World Health Organization, be it any respectful, respected big organization, takes over the whole task of standardizing by saying, "This is drug 'X.' It can have the following indication, it must have the following counter-indication." We would be more than happy to comply with that on a world-wide scale, because it would reduce our costs. It would reduce the burden of dealing with hundreds of authorities at the same time.

**RICHTER** (at WHO headquarters, Geneva): WHO officials we spoke with contend that no one in the pharmaceutical industry has ever asked WHO to take on the task of adopting uniform standards, so that everyone in the world gets the same information, the proper information, about every drug that's available on the world market.

**NARRATOR:** In the absence of any other system to reach ordinary people, the International Organization of Consumers Unions has recently helped establish a global health information network.

**ANWAR FAZAL:** Through this network now we are deliberately looking for items of news about hazardous products that might appear in different magazines in different parts of the world, in newspapers, in research done by our own organization or other agencies.

**NARRATOR:** CAP, the Consumers Association of Penang, is affiliated with the new network. CAP now alerts Malaysians to hazardous products sold in their country.

**CAP TELEPHONE OPERATOR:** Yes, you've got a complaint about a medicine?

**NARRATOR:** CAP is the most aggressive and active grass roots consumers group in the Third World. Ordinary people with complaints walk in the door to present their problems. CAP trains university students, teachers, college professors. They brief government officials, broadcast a weekly radio program, run consumer product surveys.

**EDMUND GNANAMUTHU** (CAP trainer): I described last time what dumping was. So I have here . . .

**NARRATOR:** They test the safety of some products, such as baby pacifiers.

**FOO GAIK SIM** (CAP staff): It has to have these two ventilation holes. This is just in case if the child swallows it, there are still two holes for the child to breathe. Now we've looked at Evenflo, and we found that, no doubt the size is all right, it could withstand boiling, the ventilation holes are missing. And since 1977 regulations have been passed in the States to say it has to have ventilation holes. This is clearly a case of dumping of sub-standard products into an unsuspecting country.

**NARRATOR:** CAP published a monthly newspaper which informs readers about hazardous products on the market in their part of the world. CAP does all it knows how, to warn consumers in Malaysia about drugs that have been banned or restricted for use in the western world. But they believe much more remains to be done.

**MARTIN KHOR:** We really cannot blame the consumers for taking dangerous drugs, because they just don't have the information, the counter-information as to the problems and dangers associated with these drugs. And unless such information reaches them, and unless the government takes legislative action, and the governments in the First World countries themselves stop their own companies from exporting drugs which are already banned or withdrawn or severely restricted in their own countries, the problem will just continue and probably deteriorate.

**BERNARDO KUCINSKI:** The first responsibility is the company which commits the crime deliberately. They know what a drug is about, they know what they have to write about in America, in the United States, and then they do the opposite in other countries. They omit contra-indications, they omit side effects indications, they enlarge the spectrum of indications, they falsify, scientifically falsify the image of the drug, in order to make of each drug a natural candidate to be a best-selling. They optimize the conditions, and in order to do this they falsify. They are the main responsible, because they are conscious of the crime.

**MR. PERETZ:** It isn't necessarily the manufacturer himself in the western world who's at fault, It may well be his distributor. It may well be an employee of a local agent who has no connection other than that of a buying and selling agent with the original manufacturer.

**DR. VON WARTBURG:** As far as the uses, the indications are concerned, and as far as the degree of availability is concerned, this is clearly the obligation and the responsibility by the authorities.

**RICHTER:** The pharmacist says it's the doctor's responsibility. The doctor says it's the government or it's the manufacturer's responsibility. The government says it's the manufacturers's responsibility. Now a manufacturer is saying it's the government's responsibility. Everybody is passing the buck to somebody else. How do you solve this problem?

**DR. VON WARTBURG:** I'm the first one not to ride this, what I would call "merry-go-round" of responsibilities. I think we have a

clear cut mandate, given by the nature of the business, for informing all parties, be it parties in the health care delivery system, in a
proper way. I would go on record that we try to perform that responsibility as best we can.

**DR. ALFONSO TREJOS** (Research Scientist, Costa Rica): The
multinational companies, the transnational companies have a great
deal of responsibility. But we have to be very much clear with
regard to what is their purpose, what they exist for. They exist in
order to make money to give to the stockholders.

**DR. SCHERER:** Private industry plays a major role in the development of new drugs and products that are useful for society. Unless
our society and other societies want to create entirely new public
mechanisms for drug development, we're going to have to rely on
private industry, not only to develop new drugs, but to manufacture
them, to get them out and distribute them, get them into the hands
of the people who need to use them. The fact that there are social
needs in our country, and certainly in developing countries, that
don't always correspond with the profit needs of industry, is a
tremendous problem. I think that it's a problem that our society,
and the world society is grappling with through a number of specific
efforts at the moment. The World Health Organization for some
years has been developing the concept of a basic drug list which
would identify drug products that meet health goals of the country
involved, whose costs are low.

**NARRATOR:** At the People's Health Center in Bangladesh, a new
pharmaceutical factory is being built to make essential drugs on the
World Health Organization list. Producing their own essential
medicines can free Third World countries from dependency on
transnational industry. It can also diminish some of the problems
that have come with medicines imported from the Western world.
Farhad Mazhar, marketing manager for the new factory.

**FARHAD MAZHAR:** In this place we have an idea of confronting
the multinationals, the way they are exploiting our country, the way
they are marketing the banned products. So what we want to do
here is that we want to produce the medicine which will have in
quality international standards. We'll develop the medicine by
ourselves, and then in the market we'll also come up with those
medicines which are essential for our country, which the multinational doesn't produce because it is not profitable for them. And at
the same time we'll also try to convince our people, our government,
that those banned products which the multinationals are marketing
in our country — to stop it.

**NARRATOR:** Very few Third World countries are able to build factories to produce essential drugs for their people.    Those who want to stop the exporting and misleading marketing of medicines for the Third World that are banned or restricted in our part of the world, face an enormous challenge. They will have to overcome resistance from industry and government. They will have to press for enforceable laws, country by country.

Until that happens local consumer action, linked together, seems to be the only functioning solution to this worldwide problem.

**DR. SILVERMAN:** It may not be easy to understand why Americans should be concerned by these problems. After all, not many Americans are injured by these practices. But I think we have to keep in mind that many of the companies that have been involved in these unfortunate practices are based in the United States. Many of the stockholders are Americans. We are getting money from them. And this is blood money indeed.

**ANWAR FAZAL:** Those of you who have the courage and conviction for a better society, I think should take the lead in insuring that this problem of dumping of hazardous products is eliminated from the agenda of our world.

**ON SCREEN STATEMENT:** Upjohn, which makes Depo-Provera, Albamycin-T, and Fradimicina declined to be interviewed for this report.

## CREDITS

*Produced by*
ROBERT RICHTER

*Writer/Reporter*
ROBERT RICHTER

*Associate Producer*
JACQUELINE LEOPOLD

*Cinematography*
BURLEIGH WARTES

*Editor*
PETER KINOY

*Sound:*
*Latin America*
PAMELA YATES

*Asia, Africa*
SAMANTHA HEILWEIL

*United States*
GILL McDOWELL
CHERYL GROFF

*Europe*
VLADIMIR HAVEL

*Assistant Editor*
ANNE SAHL

*Sound Editor*
ANNE SANDYS

*Research*
JACQUELINE LEOPOLD
KATHERINE GASS
SALLY GROO
JANE WARRENBRAND
JUDITH SOBOL

*Production Secretary*
SALLY GROO

*Production Liaison*
*Malaysia*
EDMUND GNANAMUTHU

*Kenya*
CARY AYUB

*Brazil*
TONY BERARDI

*Colombia*
GERARDO REYES

*Mexico*
ENRIQUE TRIGO

*Original Music*
JORDAN KAPLAN

*Special Thanks*

SMON SOSHO TOKYO CHISAI GENKOKU–DAN, TAMIKO AND CLAES BJERNER, DR. MARIAN MOSES

For WNET – *Coordinating Producer,* KATHY KLINE; *Executive Producer,* DAVID LOXTON

*This program was made possible by a grant from:* INDEPENDENT DOCUMENTARY FUND, which is supported by NATIONAL ENDOWMENT FOR THE ARTS, FORD FOUNDATION and CORPORATION FOR PUBLIC BROADCASTING

*Additional funding provided by:* FILM FUND BYDALE FOUNDATION, CS FUND, SAMUEL RUBIN FOUNDATION, UNITED NATIONS ENVIRONMENTAL PROGRAM, DANCHURCH AID, MAILMAN FOUNDATION, METHODIST BOARD OF GLOBAL MINISTRIES, OXFAM, ROCKEFELLER FAMILY ASSOCIATES, NEW LAND FOUNDATION

*and:* STEVE ALLEN, MRS. GARDNER COX, ROBERT BOYAR, CANADIAN LABOR CONGRESS, DR. MAX DELBRUCK, PAULINE STAHL SCOTT, KEN WYMAN, ACAO DEMOCRATICA FEMININA GNOCHA

*A production of* ROBERT RICHTER and the Television Laboratory at WNET/THIRTEEN

# APPENDIX II

# Appendix II

TABLE I

## The 50 Largest Transnational Pharmaceutical Companies, 1977

| Company | Domicile | Sales, Millions of dollars (a) |
|---|---|---|
| 1. Hoechst | West Germany | 1 572.9 |
| 2. Merck and Co. | United States | 1 446.4 |
| 3. Bayer | West Germany | 1 273.4 |
| 4. Ciba-Geigy | Switzerland | 1 150.0 |
| 5. Hoffmann-La Roche | Switzerland | 1 145.0 |
| 6. American Home Products | United States | 1 116.0 |
| 7. Warner-Lambert | United States | 1 024.8 |
| 8. Pfizer | United States | 1 016.0 |
| 9. Sandoz | Switzerland | 934.8 |
| 10. Eli Lilly | United States | 911.1 |
| 11. Upjohn | United States | 744.0 |
| 12. Boehringer Ingelheim | West Germany | 734.6 |
| 13. Squibb | United States | 668.4 |
| 14. Bristol Myers | United States | 666.2 |
| 15. Takeda | Japan | 645.6 |
| 16. Rhone Poulenc | France | 613.9 |
| 17. Schering-Plough | United States | 606.1 |
| 18. Glaxo | Great Britain | 594.3 |
| 19. Abbott Laboratories | United States | 581.0 |
| 20. Beecham | Great Britain | 523.8 |

| Company | Domicile | Sales, Millions of dollars (a) |
|---|---|---|
| 21. Johnson and Johnson | United States | 518.3 |
| 22. Montedison | Italy | 486.9 |
| 23. Cyanamid | United States | 484.0 |
| 24. Schering | West Germany | 456.2 |
| 25. AKZO | Netherlands | 441.5 |
| 26. ICI | Great Britain | 413.9 |
| 27. Smithkline | United states | 411.0 |
| 28. Wellcome (b) | Great Britain | 384.6 |
| 29. G.D. Searle | United States | 382.3 |
| 30. Baxter Travenol | United States | 354.6 |
| 31. Roussel Uclaf | France | 340.4 |
| 32. Revlon | United States | 333.5 |
| 33. Dow | United States | 333.0 |
| 34. Astra | Sweden | 307.2 |
| 35. Shionogi | Japan | 285.5 |
| 36. Fujisawa | Japan | 284.7 |
| 37. E. Merck | West Germany | 275.4 |
| 38. 3M | United States | 266.0 |
| 39. Sankyo | Japan | 245.0 |
| 40. Richardson Merrell | United States | 234.8 |
| 41. Sterling Drug (b) | United States | 227.5 |
| 42. Pennwalt | United States | 217.1 |
| 43. Syntex | Panama | 216.3 |
| 44. A.H. Robins | United States | 211.6 |
| 45. BASF | West Germany | 209.7 |
| 46. Mieji Seika | Japan | 174.6 |
| 47. CM Industries (b) | France | 165.4 |
| 48. Altana (formerly Varta) | West Germany | 158.4 |
| 49. Miles Laboratories | United States | 157.9 |
| 50. Tanabe Seiyaku | Japan | 153.5 |

(a) *All exchange rates to United States dollars as of 1 January 1977.*

(b) *Estimated*

Reproduced from: United Nations, Centre on Transnational Corporations. *Transnational Corporations and the Pharmaceutical Industry* (ST/CTC/9). New York: United Nations, 1979.

## TABLE II
## FOREIGN SALES TRENDS FOR 14 MAJOR
## UNITED STATES PHARMACEUTICAL COMPANIES

(Overseas sales volume as a percentage of total sales volume)

| Company | 1967 | 1971 | 1977 |
|---|---|---|---|
| 1. Merck and Company | 33 | 40 | 45 |
| 2. American Home Products | 22 | 25 | 31 |
| 3. Warner Lambert | 33 | 37 | 43 |
| 4. Pfizer | 48 | 49 | 51 |
| 5. Eli Lilly | – | 31 | 37 |
| 6. Upjohn | 26 | 34 | 37 |
| 7. Squibb | 22 | 27 | 33 |
| 8. Bristol-Myers | 17 | 18 | 31 |
| 9. Schering-Plough (a) | 39 | 34 | 43 |
| 10. Abbott | 28 | 32 | 32 |
| 11. Johnson and Johnson | 28 | 31 | 41 |
| 12. Cyanamid | 19 | 21 | 34 |
| 13. Smithkline | 20 | 26 | 36 |
| 14. Searle | 22 | 36 | 37 |

(a) *Schering Corp. and Plough, Inc. merged in 1971. The 1967 foreign sales figure is for the Schering Corp. only. The 1971 and 1977 figures are based on consolidated sales after the merger.*

Reproduced from: United Nations, Centre on Transnational Corporations. *Transnational Corporations and the Pharmaceutical Industry* (ST/CTC/9). New York: United Nations, 1979.

TABLE III
## FOREIGN SALES OF THE 50 LARGEST
## TRANSNATIONAL PHARMACEUTICAL COMPANIES, 1977
(Foreign sales volume as a percentage of total sales volume)

| Rank | Company | Percentage | Rank | Company | Percentage |
|------|---------|-----------|------|---------|-----------|
| 1. | Hoechst | 67.0 | 26. | ICI | 60.0 |
| 2. | Merck and Co. | 44.9 | 27. | Smithkline | 35.5 |
| 3. | Bayer | 69.0 | 28. | Wellcome | 86.0 |
| 4. | Ciba-Geigy | 98.0 | 29. | G.D. Searle | 37.0 |
| 5. | Hoffmann-LaRoche | 90.0 *(a)* | 30. | Baxter Travenol | 31.0 |
| 6. | American Home Products | 31.2 | 31. | Roussel Uclaf | 61.0 |
| 7. | Warner Lambert | 43.3 | 32. | Revlon | 27.7 |
| 8. | Pfizer | 51.0 | 33. | Dow | 44.6 |
| 9. | Sandoz | 95.0*(a)* | 34. | Astra | 61.0 |
| 10. | Eli Lilly | 37.0 | 35. | Shionogi | 2.0 |
| 11. | Upjohn | 37.2 | 36. | Fujiasawa | 7.0 |
| 12. | Boehringer Ingelheim | 69.0 | 37. | E. Merck | 64.5 |
| 13. | Squibb | 33.0 | 38. | 3M | 37.9 |
| 14. | Bristol Myers | 30.6 | 39. | Sankyo | 2.0 |
| 15. | Takeda | 6.0 | 40. | Richardson-Merrell | 48.4 |
| 16. | Rhone Poulenc | 59.0 | 41. | Sterling Drug | 42.0 |
| 17. | Schering-Plough | 42.9 | 42. | Pennwalt | 20.0 |
| 18. | Glaxo | 61.4 | 43. | Syntex | 45.0 *(b)* |
| 19. | Abbott Labs | 32.0 | 44. | A.H. Robins | 30.0 |
| 20. | Beecham | 70.0 | 45. | BASF | 51.0 |
| 21. | Johnson and Johnson | 41.2 | 46. | Meiji Seika | 3.0 |
| 22. | Montedison | 42.0 | 47. | CM Industries | 35.2 |
| 23. | Cyanamid | 34.0 | 48. | Altana | 35.7 |
| 24. | Schering | 63.5 | 49. | Miles Labs | 29.2 |
| 25. | AKZO | 87.7 | 50. | Tanabe Seiyaku | 6.0 |

*(a) Estimate.*

*(b) Foreign sales figure represents non-United States sales. Company headquarters are in Panama, but major production facilities are in the United States.*

Reproduced from: United Nations, Centre on Transnational Corporations. *Transnational Corporations and the Pharmaceutical Industry* (ST/CTC/9). New York: United Nations, 1979.

TABLE IV
## Direction of Pharmaceutical Exports of Major Producer Nations, 1973

| Exporting Country | Percentage Exported to | | | |
|---|---|---|---|---|
| | Latin America | Africa | Western Asia | Other Asian |
| West Germany | 22 | 13 | 22 | 25 |
| United States | 35 | 5 | 14 | 27 |
| Switzerland | 13 | 8 | 18 | 15 |
| Great Britain | 9 | 20 | 21 | 14 |
| France | 6 | 47 | 11 | 7 |
| Netherlands | 8 | 3 | 5 | 4 |
| Italy | 7 | 4 | 9 | 8 |
| Total | 100 | 100 | 100 | 100 |
| Total value (Millions dollars) | 359.5 | 379.5 | 201.5 | 459.1 |

Reproduced from: United Nations, Centre on Transnational Corporations. *Transnational Corporations and the Pharmaceutical Industry* (ST/CTC/9). New York: United Nations, 1979.

TABLE V
## Pharmaceutical Market Shares Held by Domestic and Foreign Firms in 25 Selected Countries, 1975

| Country | Domestic share Percentage | Foreign share Percentage |
|---|---|---|
| Saudi Arabia | 0 | 100 |
| Nigeria | 3 | 97 |
| Belgium | 10 | 90 |
| Venezuela | 12 | 88 |
| Canada | 15 | 85 |
| Australia | 15 | 85 |
| Brazil | 15 | 85 |
| Indonesia | 15 | 85 |
| Mexico | 18 | 82 |
| India | 25 | 75 |

| Country | Domestic share Percentage | Foreign share Percentage |
|---|---|---|
| Iran | 25 | 75 |
| Argentina | 30 | 70 |
| Philippines | 35 | 65 |
| Italy *(a)* | 40 | 60 |
| Netherlands *(a)* | 40 | 60 |
| South Africa | 40 | 60 |
| United Kingdom *(a)* | 40 | 60 |
| Sweden *(a)* | 50 | 50 |
| France *(a)* | 55 | 45 |
| Spain | 55 | 45 |
| Germany, Federal Republic of *(a)* | 65 | 35 |
| Switzerland *(a)* | 72 | 28 |
| United States *(a)* | 85 | 15 |
| Japan *(a)* | 87 | 13 |
| USSR | 100 | 0 |

*(a) The home country of at least one of the major pharmaceutical transnational corporations.*

Reproduced from: United Nations, Centre on Transnational Corporations. *Transnational Corporations and the Pharmaceutical Industry* (ST/CTC/9). New York: United Nations, 1979.

TABLE VI
DOUBLE STANDARD CASES

| Industry | Location | Type of Hazard Reported | Multinational Affiliation | Type of Affiliaton | Ref No. |
|---|---|---|---|---|---|
| Asbestos milling | South Africa | Children with severe asbestosis | Cape Asbestos (U.K.) | Subsidiary mining operation | 18 |
| Alpha-naphthylamine manufacture | (Outside of the U.K.) | Bladder cancer | Imperial Chemical Industries (U.K.) | Not known | 5 |
| Benzidine dye manufacture | (outside of the U.K.) | Bladder cancer | – – | – – | 10 |
| Asbestos textile manufacture | Agua Prieta and and Juarez, Mexico | Not informing workers, not providing clothes change, neighborhood pollution | Amatex (U.S.) | Subsidiary | 10 |
| Trichlorophenol manufacture | Saveso, Italy | Workplace and air pollution with dioxins, failure to inform workers, inadequate safety controls in plant design | Givaudan of Hoffman La-Roche (Switzerland) | Subsidiary | 10 |
| Asbestos friction product and textile manufacture | Bombay, India | Numerous workplace hazards uncontrolled, failure to inform workers of the hazard and to tell them of medical exam findings | Turner and Newall, Ltd., (U.K.) | 74% ownership | 9,12 |
| Asbestos | Countries without labeling requirements | Failure to affix warning labels | Entire asbestos industry (Asbestos International Association) | – – | 12,15 |

| Process | Location | Hazard | Company | Relationship | Ref. |
|---|---|---|---|---|---|
| Asbestos cement manufacture | Ahmedabad, India | Water pollution, solid waste dumping, no warnings on products | Johns-Manville (U.S.) | Minority ownership, exclusive marketing of exports, raw material sales, plant design and construction supervision | 3,8 |
| Asbestos brake lining manufacture | Madras, India | Solid waste dumping | Cape Industries (U.K.) | 25% ownership | 9 |
| Asbestos brake shoe manufacture | South Korea | Substandard working conditions | Not known | – – | 4 |
| Asbestos textiles | Republic of South Africa | – – | Deutsche Kap-Asbestwerke | Subsidiary | 2 |
| Asbestos milling | Quebec, Canada | Lack of work-place dust controls | Asbestos Corp., Ltd. of General Dynamics (U.S.) | Subsidiary | 19 |
| Asbestos brake shoe | Cork, Ireland | Newly built brake shoe manufacturing plant utilizing asbestos as raw material | Raybestos-Manhattan (U.S.) | Subsidiary | 13 |
| Epoxy spraying | (Shipyards outside of Denmark) | Eczema, cancer (?) | Not known | – – | 1 |
| Chromate and dichromate manufacture | Lecheria, Mexico | Waste dumping, workplace exposures producing nasal septum perforation | Bayer (W. Germany) | Partial ownership | 14,16 |

| Dye manufacture | Bombay, India | Water pollution | Montedison (Italy) | Partial ownership | 16 |
|---|---|---|---|---|---|
| Mercury cell chlorine plant | Managua, Nicaragua | Mercury poisoning, water pollution | Pennwalt Corp. (U.S.) | 40% ownership and management of the plant | 11,20 |
| Steelmaking | Malaysia | Air pollution, workplace hazards | Nippon Steel (Japan) | Minority ownership and plant design | 6 |
| Polyvinyl chloride manufacture | Malaysia | High worker exposure to (carcinogen) vinyl chloride | "Japanese companies" | Partial ownership | 6 |
| Arsenical pesticides manufacture | Malaysia | Arsenic poisoning symptoms in workers, no monitoring of exposure | Diamond Shamrock (U.S.) | Subsidiary | 6 |
| Paint, pesticide, and metal plating wastes | Latin America | Waste dumping | Not known | – – | 17 |
| Polychlorinated biphenyls and other chemical wastes | Zacatecas, Mexico | Waste dumping | Diamond Shamrock, B.F. Goodrich, and Monochem (all U.S.) | Waste disposal agent for large U.S. firms | 7 |

Reproduced from: Castleman, Barry, I. "The 'Double Standard' in Industrial Control of Health Hazards." Paper presented at Section of Environmental Sciences and Public Policy, New York Academy of Sciences, 4 February 1981.

# References for Table VI

1. R. Ahlberg (International Metalworkers Federation), *IMF Bulletin on Occupational Health and Safety No. 4,* Geneva, April 1979.

2. Anon., *Asbestos* 61 (January 1980): 30

3. Anon., "Canada: Lean Now But Future Bright," *Asbestos* 62 (January 1981): 12-13.

4. Anon., "Nicht Sittenwidrig," *Stern,* 19 June 1980.

5. Anon., "Plant Shut for Health Reasons," *The Guardian,* 27 November 1965.

6. R. Belmar, "Information Supplementing the Report on Mercury Poisoning in Nicaragua Published in Morbidity and Mortality Weekly Report, August 22, 1980" (New York: Montefiore Hospital and Medical Center, n.d.)

7. R. Blumenthal, "Mexico Jails American on Charge He Imported U.S. Chemical Wastes," *New York Times,* 20 March 1981.

8. Barry I. Castleman, *Cancer Causing Chemicals* (New York: Van Nostrand Reinhold, 1981).

9. Barry I. Castleman, "Double Standards: Asbestos in India," *New Scientist* 89 (26 February 1981): 522-523.

10. Barry I. Castleman, "The Export of Hazardous Factories to Developing Nations," *International Journal of Health Services* 9 (1979): 569-606.

11. Barry I. Castleman, "Reply to Levenstein and Eller," *International Journal of Health Services* 11 (1981): 311-313.

12. Barry I. Castleman and M.J. Vera Vera, "Impending Proliferation of Asbestos," *International Journal of Health Services* 10 (1980): 389-403.

13. T. MacSweeney, "Controversial U.S. Asbestos Firm Pulls Out of Ireland," *World Environment Report* 6 (17 November 1980): 1.

14. M.A. Mendoza, "La Muerta Fra un Polvo Amarillo sobre Lecheria," *Excelsior,* 20 October 1976.

15. R. Osborne, "Cutting the Asbestos Risk," *Far Eastern Economic Review,* (22 August 1980) pp. 73-74.

16. M.R. Redondo, "Perforacion del Tabique Nasal en 46% del Personal de la Fabrica," *Excelsior,* 6 June 1978.

17. B. Richards, "Sierra Leone Rejects Chemical Waste Plan," *Washington Post,* 22 February 1980.

18. G.W.H. Schepers, "Discussion," *Annals of the New York Academy of Science* 132 (1965): 246-247.

19. L. Tataryn, Dying for a Living (n.p., Canada: Greenberg Publications, Ltd., 1979), p. 54.

# REFERENCE AND SOURCE NOTES

## Chapter I

1. United Nations Conference on Trade and Development (UNCTAD), *Handbook of International Trade and Development Statistics,* Supplement 1979, 1980, February 1981.

2. U.S. Congress, *Export of Hazardous Products,* Hearing before the Subcommittee on International Economic Policy and Trade, House of Representatives, June 5, 12 and September 9, 1980 (Washington, D.C.: U.S. Government Printing Office, 1980).

3. Susan B. King, Chairman, U.S. Consumer Product Safety Commission, "U.S. Export of Banned Products." Hearings before the U.S. Congress, Subcommittee on Commerce, Consumer and Monetary Affairs, House of Representatives, July 11, 12, and 13, 1978 (Washington, D.C.: U.S. Government Printing Office, 1978).

4. Wolfgang Howorka, *Dangerous Drugs,* Consumer Action for Developing Countries (January 1980).

5. a) Bill Richards, "U.S. Fights Export of Hazardous Waste," *Washington Post,* 26 January, 1980.

    b) Barry J. Castleman, "The Back Door is Open for Chemical Wastes," *Dangerous Properties of Industrial Materials Report,* (November/December 1980): 2-4.

6. Henry M. Leicester, *The Historical Background of Chemistry* (New York: Dover Publishing, Inc., 1971).

7. Louis Vaczek, *The Enjoyment of Chemistry* (New York: The Viking Press, 1964).

8. a) Jules Backman, *Chemicals in the National Economy,* (Washington, D.C.: Manufacturing Chemists Assoc., 1964).

    b) U.S. Department of Commerce, Business and Defense Services Administration. *Chemicals, Quarterly Industry Report.* March, 1965-1972.

    c) Organization for Economic Cooperation and Development (OECD) *The Chemical Industry: 1979* (Paris: OECD, 1981).

9. Organization for Economic Cooperation and Development (OECD). *The Chemical Industry: 1974/75* (Paris: OECD, 1976).

10. Food and Agriculture Organization, *Trade Year Book, 1979* (Rome, Italy: FAO-UN, Vol. 33).

11. "Poisons and Peripheral People: Hazardous Substances in the Third World," *Newsletter* (Cambridge, Mass.: Cultural Survival, Inc., Summer, 1981).

12. U.S. Department of Agriculture (USDA), *The Pesticide Review*, 1979 (Washington, D.C.: USDA).

13. U.S. General Accounting Office, *Better Regulation of Pesticide Exports and Pesticide Residues in Imported Foods is Essential* (Washington, D.C.: U.S. Government Printing Office, 1979).

14. *1978 Yearbook of International Trade Statistics*, Volume 2: Trade by Commodity (New York: United Nations, 1979).

15. United Nations Center on Transnational Corporations (UNCTC), *Transnational Corporations and the Pharmaceutical Industry* (New York: UNCTC, 1979).

16. Michael Bader, "Hustling Drugs to the Third World," *The Progressive* (December 1979), p. 42-46.

17. *The Food and Drug Letter*, July 17, 1981 (Washington, D.C.: Washington Business Information, Inc.).

18. "Background Report on Executive Order 12264 on Federal Policy Regarding the Export of Banned or Significantly Restricted Substances," *Federal Register*, Vol. 46, p. 7806-7820 (January 23, 1981).

19. Sanjaya Lall, "Medicines and Multinationals: Problems of the Transfer of Pharmaceutical Technology to the Third World," *Monthly Review*, March 1977, pp. 20-30.

20. Anil Agarwal, *Drugs and the Third World* (London: Earthscan, 1978).

21. United Nations Conference on Trade and Development (UNCTAD), *Major Issues in the Transfer of Technology to Developing Countries: A Case Study of the Pharmaceutical Industry* (Geneva: United Nations, 1975).

# Chapter II

1. *Farm Chemicals Handbook* (Willoughby, Ohio: Meister Publishing Co., 1980).

2. George Waldbott, *Health Effects of Environmental Pollutants*, 2nd ed. (St. Louis: C.V. Mosby Co., 1978).

3. Marion Moses, "Pesticides," draft to be published in *Environmental and Occupational Medicine*, ed. William Rom and Jeff Lee, 1981, Mimeographed.

4. Amos Turk, Jonathan Turk, Janet Wittes and Robert Wittes, *Environmental Science*, 2nd ed. (Philadelphia: W.B. Saunders, 1978).

5. Erick Eckholm and Jacob Scherr, "Double Standards and the Pesticide Trade," *New Scientist* 77 (16 February 1978): 441-443.

6. "Egyptians Killed by Pesticide," *Washington Post*, 10 December 1976.

7. Alan Riding, "Free Use of Pesticides in Guatamala Takes Its Toll," *New York Times*, 9 November 1977.

8. "Profit and Poison in Guatemala," *New York Times*, 19 November 1977.

9. U.S., Council on Environmental Quality, *Environmental Quality 1978: The Ninth Annual Report of the Council on Environmental Quality* (Washington, D.C.: United States Government Printing Office, 1978).

10. United Nations, World Health Organization, "Pesticides in Use for Public Health," *WHO Chronicle* 32 (1978): 339-344.

11. Loretta McLaughlin, "Concern Is Growing in Peru Over Use of Banned Chemicals," *World Environment Report*, 8 October 1979.

12. Wirasak Sakyakanond, "Thai Savant Sounds Warning on Excessive Pesticide Contamination," *Depthnews Science Service*, Press Foundation of Asia, DNSS no. 204-79, August 1979.

13. Dave Bull, "Third World Health Hazards Linked to British Exports," *Oxfam Public Affairs Unit Newsletter*, London, 5 December 1980.

14. U.S., Council on Environmental Quality, *Environmental Quality 1975: The Sixth Annual Report of the Council on Environmental Quality* (Washington, D.C.: United States Government Printing Office, 1975).

15. David Weir and Mark Shapiro, *Circle of Poison* (San Francisco Institute for Food and Development Policy, 1981).

16. U.S. Environmental Protection Agency, Office of Public Awareness, *Suspended and Cancelled Pesticides*, OPA 159/9, October 1979.

17. *40 Code of Federal Regulations*, Section 162.31, July 1980.

18. U.S. Environmental Protection Agency, Office of Pesticide Programs, *Recognition and Management of Pesticide Poisoning*, 2nd ed. (Washington, D.C.: United States Government Printing Office, 1977).

19. "Pesticides Banned in U.S. Being Used in Kenya," *Daily Nation* (Kenya), 26 October 1980.

20. J. Bennet, "A Comparison of Selected Methods and a Test of the Pre-Adaptive Hypothesis," *Heredity* 15 (1960): 65-77.

21. United Nations, United Nations Environment Programme, Dr. Mostaga Kamal Toba, Executive Director, *State of the World Environment 1979: Report of the Executive Director of the United Nations Environment Programme*, 1979.

22. E. Chanlett, *Environmental Protection* (New York: McGraw Hill, 1973).

23. Penny Lernoux, "Colombia Mounts Major Study of Excessive Pesticide Use," *World Environment Report*, 15 January 1979, pp. 4-5.

24. Charles E. Warren, "Feeling Uncle Sam's Actions Abroad," *Washington Post*, 6 February 1978.

25. Georganne Chapin and Robert Wasserstrom, "A Bitter Harvest," *Progressive*, March 1980, pp. 31-34.

26. R. Jeffrey Smith, "U.S. Beginning to Act on Banned Pesticides," *Science* 204 (29 June 1979): 1391-1394.

27. U.S., Government Accounting Office, *Better Regulations of Pesticide Exports and Pesticide Residues in Imported Foods Is Essential* (Washington D.C.: United States Government Printing Office, 22 June 1979).

28. Bob Richter, Interview with Ian Nesbit, Office of Clements Associates, Washington, D.C., 2 July 1981.

29. "Company President Gets Six Months, $2000 Fine For Illegal Pesticide Sales," *Chemical Regulation Reporter* 7 (12 June 1981): 242.

30. News Release, Wisconsin Senator Gaylord Nelson, Washington, D.C., 30 January 1978.

31. Laurie Becklund and Ronald B. Taylor, "Toxic Residues Halts Tomatoes Bound For U.S.," *Los Angeles Times*, 16 March 1980.

32. U.S., Congress, House, Committee on Foreign Affairs, *Export of Hazardous Products: Hearings Before the Subcommittee on International Economic Policy and Trade.* 96th Congress, 2nd session, 5, 12 June and 9 September 1980.

33. Frank Penna, *Policy Issues on Appropriate Pesticide Technology: A Briefing Paper* (New York City: The Policy Sciences Center, Inc., 31 March 1978).

34. U.S. Council on Environmental Quality, *Environmental Quality 1976: The Seventh Annual Report of the Council on Environmental Quality* (Washington, D.C.: United States Government Printing Office, 1976).

35. Joanne Omang, "Park Service to Stop 2,4-D Weedkiller Use on All Its 325 Areas," *Washington Post,* 15 November 1980.

36. Penny Lernoux, "Columbian Scientists Charge Government Fails to Control Toxic Chemicals," *World Environment Report,* 2 January 1978.

37. U.S. State Department and the U.S. National Committee for Man and the Biosphere, "Statement of Mr. Samuel Gitonga," *Proceedings of the U.S. Strategy Conference on Pest Management,* Washington, D.C., 7-8 June 1979.

38. Ronald B. Taylor, "DBCP Still Used Despite Dangers" in *The Poisoning of America,* reprints from *The Los Angeles Times,* 28 June 1979.

39. U.S., Environmental Protection Agency, Office of Pesticide Programs, *Pesticide Protection: A Training Manual for Health Personnel,* (Washington, D.C.: United States Government Printing Office, March 1977).

40. Personal Communication, Dr. Fred Whittimore, Association for International Development (USAID), Agricultural Office, 30 September 1981.

41. Environmental Protection Agency response to NRDC Freedom of Information request, 18 December 1980.

42. Bob Richter transcripts of TV Series: see *Appendix.*

# Chapter III

1. U.S. Department of Health, Education, and Welfare, Public Health Service, "DESI/Drug Efficacy Study Implementation/Study," FDA/Food and Drug Administration/Talk Paper, 3 April 1980.

2 . U.S. Agency for International Development, Office of Public Affairs (Peggy Streit, ed.), *World Development Letter* 3, no. 9 (29 April 1980), pp. 34-35.

3. Khor Kok Peng, "Penang Consumer's Assocciation," *The Centre Report* IV, no. 4 (December 1979).

4. Gary Herbertson, "NGOs in Cooperation with UNEP," *The Centre Report* IV, no. 4 (December 1979), p. 8.

5. Lynne McTaggart, "Putting Drug Testers to the Test," *New York Times Magazine,* 7 December 1980, pp. 174-180.

6. Van Woert, "High Cost of America's Drug Approval Standard," Letter dated 18 June 1980 to the editor of The *New York Times.*

7. Wayne L. Pines, "Drugs: A Consumer Advocate's View," *FDA Consumer,* December 1978-January 1979, pp. 10-15.

8. John S. Yudkin, "Provision of Medicines in a Developing Country," *The Lancet,* 15 April 1978, pp. 810-812.

9. Oliver Gillie, "Hazardous Drugs Sold For Use in Africa by International Companies," *London Sunday Times,* 13 August 1978, p. 8.

10. Mark Dowie, "The Corporate Crime of the Century," *Mother Jones*, November 1979, p. 23; B. Ehrenreich and Mark Dowie, "The Charge: Gynocide, The Accused: The U.S. Government," *Mother Jones*, November 1979, p. 26; David Weir, Mark Shapiro and Terry Jacobs, "The Boomerang Crime," *Mother Jones*, November 1979.

11. Olle Hansson, "The Consumers Voice," Paper read at the Kyoto (Japan) International Conference Against Drug-induced Sufferings, 13-18 April 1979.

12. Leslie Wolf, "Bristol-Myer's 'Third World' Cancer Cure," *Multinational Monitor*, March, 1980

13. Jeremy Bugler, "Drugs: Rich Man, Poor Man . . ." (London: Earthscan, 1979).

14. World Health Organization, "The Selection of Essential Drugs," Report of a WHO Expert Committee, WHO Technical Report Series no. 615, Geneva, Switzerland, n.d.

15. "Drugs in Pregnancy, *The Medical Letter* 14 (1972).

16. Michael Bader, "Hustling Drugs to the Third World; 'Let the Buyer Beware'," *The Progressive*, December 1979, pp. 42-46.

17. Wolfgang Howorka, "Dangerous Drugs," *Consumer Action for Developing Countries*, January 1980. (A Publication of the International Organization of Consumers Unions (IOCU), The Hague, Netherlands.)

18. T.N. Ninan, "Drugs: A Look Back Becomes a Step Forward," Earthscan press release, 1980, London, England.

19. "A Critical Look at the Drug Industry; How Profit Distorts Medicine," (Chicago, Illinois: Rush Medical School, n.d.).

20. Charles Medawar, "Drug Multinationals , Dangerous Drugs and the WHO," preprint of an article, n.d.

21. U.S. Congress, House, Committee on Foreign Affairs, *Export of Hazardous Products: Hearings Before The Subcommittee on International Economic Policy and Trade*, 96th Cong., 2nd sess., 5 and 12 June, and 9 September 1980.

22. *Ibid.* Statement of Anwar Fazal, President of IOCU.

23. *Ibid.* Statement of Dr. Pramilla Senanayake, Medical Program Advisor, International Planned Parenthood Federation.

24. *Ibid.* Statement of Roger Rochat, Representative of the Ad Hoc Consultative Panel on Depot Medroxyprogesterone Acetate.

25. *Ibid.* Statement of Gordon Duncan, Manager, Scientific Liaison, The UpJohn Company.

26. *Ibid.* Statement of Steven Minkin, Health Policy Analyst, National Women's Health Network.

27. United Nations Centre on Transnational Corporations (UNCTC), *Transnational Corporations and the Pharmaceutical Industry*, Report No. ST/CTC/9 (New York: United Nations, 1979).

28. Bill Breckon, "In Sickness or in Wealth," Transcript of Part I of two "on the spot" reports, transmitted 26 August 1979, Radio 4, British Broadcasting Corporation (BBC), England.

29. Robert Richter, Notes from interview with Mr. Matenga, Chief Pharmacist, Nairobi, Kenya, 26 June 1980.

30. Milton Roewer, *Comparative National Policies in Health Care* (New York: Marcel Dekker, Inc., 1977).

31. F. Lobo to Robert Richter, 6 February 1980.

152    PILLS, PESTICIDES & PROFITS

32. E.C. Gooding, College Medical Officer, Fourah Bay College, Sierra Leone to Judy Norsigian, Boston Women's Health Collective, Inc., 27 April 1979.

33. Roselyne Owino, Family Planning Midwife, Kisomo, Kenya to Judy Norsigian, 8 July 1979.

34. Winifred Amene, to Robert Richter, 27 March 1980.

35. Mushtagul Huq, "Health Problems and Programs in Bangladesh – An Overview" (Paper presented at the Population, Health and Development Course organized by the Population Study Centre (PSC) of the Bangladesh Institute of Development Studies, in collaboration with the National Institute of Population Research and Training (NIPORT) of the Ministry of Health and Population Control, and the Economic Development Institute (EDI) of the World Bank, 7 July to 7 August, 1980).

36. Renee Ford, "Pharmaceutical Drug Company Practices in the Labelling and Promotion of Prescription Drugs Sold in Foreign Countries," (Report prepared for the Science Policy Research Division, Congressional Research Service, for Select Committee on Small Business, Subcommittee on Monopoly, U.S. Senate, 1 March 1980).

37. Milton Silverman, *The Drugging of the Americas* (Berkeley and Los Angeles: University of California Press, 1976).

38. Dorothy Kweyu, "Medicines with Dangerous Compounds on Market," *Sunday Nation* (Nairobi, Kenya) 20 April 1980.

39. Personal communication, Aida LeRoy, Health Information Designs, Inc., Washington, D.C ., 8 June 1981.

40. Silvestre Frenk, Instituto Mexicano del Seguro Social. Interview with Robert Richter, 14 April 1980.

41. Cesar G. Victora, 'Drug Promotion in Brazil: A Study of Biased Advertising Practices," (Publication of the School of Medicine, Universidade Federal de Pelotas, November 1978).

42. Personal communication, Judith Krauss, U.S. Food and Drug Administration, Consumer and Professional Relations Staff, 4 May 1981.

43. Martin Schweiger, M.B., Ch.B., Medical Advisor/Administrator, Rangpur Dinajpur Rehabilitation Service Health Program, Lalmanirhat-Rangpur, Bangladesh, to Robert Richter, 20 May 1980.

44. Transcript of interview with Carol Yates in documentary film produced by Belbo Films, Ltd., London, England, 1981.

45. Transcript of interview with Dr. John Yudkin in documentary film produced by Belbo Films, Ltd., London, England, 1981.

46. Personal communication, Jay Kingham, Vice-President, Pharmaceutical Manufacturers Association (PMA), International Division, 30 April 1981.

47. William Breckon, "In sickness or in Wealth: Pharmaceuticals in the Third World," Transcript of Part II of two parts, transmitted 2 September 1979, Radio 4, British Broadcasting Corporation (BBC), England.

48. Janice Grange, Health Sister, Kota Belud, Sabah, East Malaysia, to Jacqueline Leopold, Richter-McBride, Inc., New York, 23 September 1980.

49. Robert Richter, "Pesticides and Pills: For Export Only." Transcript of documentary film, June 1981.

50. Personal communication, Robert Schafer, Sterling Drug company, New York, 30 April 1981.

51. Personal communication, James Russo, Director of Government and Industry Affairs, Smith Kline & French Corporation, Philadelphia, 29 April 1981.

52. Minutes from the Symposium on Epidemiological Issues in Reported Drug-induced Illness – Subacute Mylo-Optic Neuropathy (SMON) and Other Examples, 19-21 January 1976, Honolulu, Hawaii.

53. John S. Yudkin, "The Economics of Pharmaceutical Supply in Tanzania," *International Journal of Health Services* 10 (1980): 455-477.

54. David Kay, *International Regulation of Pharmaceutical Drugs*, A report to the National Science Foundation on the Application of International Regulatory Techniques to Scientific/Technical Problems, American Society of International Law Policy No. 14 (Washington, D.C.: West Publishing Company, 1976).

55. Jonathan Kandell, "Drug Marketers Stir Bitter Debate in Brazil," *New York Times*, 14 November 1976.

56. Charles Medawar, *Insult or Injury, An Inquiry into the Marketing and Advertising of British Food and Drug Products in the Third World* (London: Social Audit, Ltd., 1979).

57. Thomas C. Hayes, "The Drug Business Sees a Golden Era Ahead," *New York Times*, 17 May 1981.

58. American Medical Association (AMA), Department of Drugs, *AMA Drug Evaluations*, 4th ed. (Chicago: American Medical Association, 1980).

59. Alfred Goodman Gilman, Louis S. Gilman, and Alfred Gilman , eds., *The Pharmacological Basis of Therapeutics*, 6th edition (New York: Macmillan Publishing Company, 1980).

60. *Physicians Desk Reference*, 35th Edition (Oradell, New Jersey: Litton Industries, Inc., 1981).

61. Personal communication, Consumer and Professional Relations Staff, U.S. Food and Drug Administration, Washington, D.C., 30 June 1981.

62. D.D. Varonos, S. Santamouris, and S. Karambali, "The Incidence of Dipyrone-induced Agranulocytosis in Greece During 1975," *Journal of International Medical Research* 7 (1979): 564-568.

63. Organizing Committee of the Geneva Press Conference on SMON, *Geneva Press Conference on SMON*, Proceedings of the Geneva Press Conference on SMON, 28 April 1980, Geneva, Switzerland (Tokyo: Organizing Committee of the Geneva Press Conference on SMON, 1980).

64. M. Dunne, M. Flood, and A. Herxheimer, "Clioquinol: Availability and Instructions for Use," *Journal of Antimicrobial Chemotherapy* 2 (1976): 21-29.

65. Harold J. Simon, "Pharmaceuticals for Developing Countries: An Interface of Science, Technology, and Public Policy," *The Pharos*, Spring 1981, pp. 9-15.

66. C.E. Gordon Smith, "Major Disease Problems in the Developing World," (Paper delivered at Conference on Pharmaceuticals for Developing Countries, National Academy of Sciences, Institute of Medicine, Division of International Health, Washington, D.C., 1979).

67. International Federation of Pharmaceutical Manufacturers Association (IFPMA), "Policy Statement on International Labelling of Prescription Medicines," (Resolution adopted by IFPMA Council, 11 November 1976).

68. *Ibid.* "IFPMA Code of Pharmaceutical Marketing Practices," (Zurich: IFPMA, April 1981).

69. Pharmaceutical Manufacturers Association (PMA), News Release, (Washington, D.C.: PMA, 13 April 1981).

70. The UpJohn Company, News Release on Depo-Provera, (Washington, D.C.: The UpJohn Company, 9 September 1980).

71. Poura P. Bhiwandiwala, "Contraceptives Save Lives," manuscript submitted to *Mother Jones,* 1979.

72. Walter von Wartburg, Director of Pharmapolicy, Ciba-Geigy, Basel, Switzerland. Transcript of interview with Robert Richter, Richter-McBride Productions, July, 1981.

73. Michael Peretz, Executive Vice-President, International Federation of Pharmaceutical Manufacturers Associations. Transcript of interview with Robert Richter, July, 1981.

74. Abel Gonzalez-Cortes, *et. al.* "Typhoid Fever Follow Up — Mexico, 1974." *Morbidity and Mortality Weekly Report* (26 April, 1975): 155-56.

75. Lars L. Gustafsson, and Katarina Wide. "Marketing of Obsolete Antibiotics in Central America." *The Lancet* (3 January, 1981): 31-33.

76. Douglas H. Huber, MD, Assistant Professor, Department of Gynecology and Obstetrics, Johns Hopkins University School of Medicine. Letter to the editor, *Washington Post,* 5 April, 1980.

77. Paul J. Edelson, MD, Assistant Professor of Pediatrics, Harvard Medical School. Personal communication, June, 1981.

78. Press Release, International Plasmid Conference, Boston, Massachusetts, 4 August, 1981.

79. Walsh McDermott. "Pharmaceuticals: Their Role in Developing Societies." *Science* 209 (1980): 240-45.

80. *African Monthly Index of Medical Specialties.* Volume 20, No. 7, July 1980.

81. *Federal Register,* 1 February 1972, p. 2460

# Chapter IV

1. H. Dewar, "Agencies Announce Steps to Restrict a Pesticide," Washington *Post,* 9 September, 1977.

2. Barry I. Castleman, "The Export of Hazardous Factories to Developing Nations," *The International Journal of Health Services* 9, no. 4 (1979): 569-606.

3. Barry I. Castleman and Manual J. Vera Vera, "Impending Proliferation of Asbestos," *The International Journal of Health Services* 10, no. 3 (1980): 389-403.

4. Barry Newman, "Danger at Work," *Wall Street Journal,* 9 December 1980.

5. Neil Maxwell, "Health Issue: How Johns-Manville Mounts Counterattack in Asbestos Dispute," *Wall Street Journal,* 30 June 1980.

6. Barry I. Castleman, "Double Standards: Asbestos in India," *New Scientist,* 26 February 1981, pp. 522-23.

7. Barry I. Castleman, Letter to the Editor in response to Levenstein-Eller Critique, *International Journal of Health Services* 11, (1981): 311-13.

8. Barry I. Castleman, Rakesh Madan and Robert Mayes, "Industrial Hazards Exported to India," *Economic and Political Weekly* 16, 13 June 1981, pp. 1057-58.

9. R. B. Taylor, "Production of Highly Toxic Pesticide Shifts to Mexico," Los Angeles *Times,* 9 September, 1978.

10. "Mexico Shuts Down DBCP Production," *Toxic Material News,* 13 December, 1978.

11. McGraw-Hill Publishing Company, Economics Department, "Investment for Air and Water Pollution Control." *in* "22nd Annual Survey of Overseas Operations of US Industrial Companies, 1980-82." (New York: McGraw-Hill, 1980.)

12. US Department of Commerce. Records for import commodity, TSUSA No. 518.2100.

13. R.K. Rangan, "Proof of Cancer Among Men in Asbestos Units," The *Times* of India, 27 March, 1981.

14. P. Sweeney, "Juarez Plant a 'Runaway' Firm?" El Paso *Times,* 4 April, 1978.

15. R. A. Clifton, "Asbestos in 1980," US Department of the Interior, Washington, DC, 1980.

16. "Canada: Lean Now but Future Bright," *Asbestos* 62 (January 1981): 12-13.

17. Industrial Union Department, AFL-CIO, "National Stewardship: Unilateral International Regulation of Occupational and Environmental Hazards," Washington, DC: AFL-CIO, 29 September, 1980

18. S. Jacob Scherr, Natural Resources Defense Council. Testimony before the Subcommittee on International Economic Policy and Trade of the House Foreign Affairs Committee, *Export of Hazardous Products,* 96th US Congress, 2nd Session, 5, 12 June and 9 September, 1980.

19. "Severe mercury poisoning of both Lake Managua and chemical workers has been attributed to an American multinational chemical firm by the Sandinista government," *Environment* 23 (September 1981): 21-22.

20. Bill Richards, "U.S. Fights Export of Hazardous Waste," *Washington Post,* 26 January 1980.

21. U.S. Department of State, Unclassified Outgoing Telegram to Freetown, Sierra Leone on the "Disposal of Toxic Waste in Sierra Leone," 17 January 1980.

22. Environmental Protection Agency, "Hazardous Waste Fact Sheet," *EPA Journal,* 1979. Cited in Natural Resources Defense Council, *NRDC World Environment Alert* (Washington: NRDC, 29 January 1980).

23. Natural Resources Defense Council, "Proposed Disposal of U.S. Toxic Wastes in West Africa," *NRDC World Environment Alert* (Washington: NRDC, 29 January 1980).

24. U.S. Congress, House, Committee on Foreign Affairs, *Export of Hazardous Products: Hearings Before the Subcommittee on International Economic Policy and Trade,* 96th Congress, 2nd Session, 5, 12 June and 9 September 1980.

25. *Ibid.* Prepared statement of Faith T. Campbell, Research Associate, International Project, Natural Resources Defense Council, Inc.

26. John B. Craig, First Secretary, Chief, Economic/Commercial Section, Embassy of the United States of America, Port-au-Prince, Haiti. Letter to S. Jacob Scherr, Natural Resources Defense Council, Inc., Washington, D.C., July 1980.

27. Dan Weisman, "Toxic Wastes May Find Way to Haitian Sites," *Sunday Star-Ledger* (Newark, N.J.), 10 February 1980.

28. Michael Isikoff, "D.C. Plans to Ship Sludge to Haiti; State Dept. Fears 'Image' Problem," *Washington Star,* 21 April 1980.

29. Eugene Robinson, "Antigua Weighs Offer of D.C. Sludge," *Washington Post,* 29 July 1980.

30. Michael Isikoff, "Area Sludge Trip Cancelled in Wake of Antigua Protest," *Washington Star,* 13 September 1980.

31. "Alabama and E.P.A. to Examine Company's Waste Disposal Plan," *New York Times*, 28 December 1980.

32. "Company Seeking to Ship Toxic Waste to Bahamas," *New York Times*, 19 January 1981.

33. Ralph Blumenthal, "Mexico Jails American on Charge He Imported U.S. Chemical Wastes," *New York Times*, 20 March 1981.

34. Barry I. Castleman, "The Back Door is Open for Chemical Wastes," *Dangerous Properties of Industrial Materials Report*, November/December 1980, pp. 2-4.

35. National Research Council, *Polychlorinated Biphenyls – Report Prepared by the Committee on the Assessment of Polychlorinated Biphenyls in the Environment*(Washington, D.C.: National Academy of Sciences, 1979).

36. "Waste Export Incident Causes U.S. Policy Reappraisal," *Hazardous Waste Report* 2, no. 18 (March 1981).

37. U.S. Department of State, Unclassified Outgoing Telegram to all OECD [Organization for Economic Cooperation and Development] Capitals on the "Export of Hazardous (Non-nuclear) Wastes," Washington, D.C., 10 February 1980.

38. P. György, "Human milk and resistance to infection." in *Nutrition and Infection,* edited by G. E. W. Wolstenholme and M. O'Connor. Ciba Foundation Study Group No. 31, London, 1967. (cited in 42)

39. R.R. Puffer, and Serrano, C. V. *Patterns of Mortality in Childhood.* Washington, DC: Pan-American Health Organization, 1973. (cited in 42)

40. F. Mönckeberg, "Factors conditioning malnutrition in Latin America, with special reference to Chile." *Bibl. Nutr. Dieta* No. 14 (1970): 23-33. (cited in 42)

41. Douglas A. Johnson, of Infant Formula Action Coalition (INFACT). Fundraising letter, undated.

42. Michael B. Bader, "Breast feeding: the Role of Multinational Corporations in Latin America." *International Journal of Health Services* 6 (1976): 609-26.

43. Douglas Johnson, Chairperson, INFACT. Testimony before Subcommittee on Foreign Economic Policy and Trade. 30 Janaury, 1980.

44. M. Adinolfi, and Alan Glynn. "The Interaction of Antibacterial factors in breast milk." *Develop. Med. and Child Neurol.* 21 (1979): 808-10.

45. Derrick B. Jelliffe and E.F. Patrice Jelliffe. "Human milk, nutrition, and the world resource crisis." *Science* 188 (May 9, 1975): 557-61.

46. Robert Reinhold. "Furor Over Baby Formulas – Where, When, and How." New York *Times*, 24 May, 1981.

47. Judy Mann. "Dying Babies: America and the Third World." Washington *Post*, 22 May, 1981.

48. Boyce Rensberger. "Drop in Breast Feeding Causes Problems in Poor Countries." New York *Times*, 6 April, 1976.

49. Lydia Chavez. "Baby Formula Makers Unfazed." New York *Times*, 22 May, 1981.

50. Michael C. Latham, M.D. "THe Dase Against Nestlé." Statement before the Governing Board, National Council of Churches, New York, 3 November, 1978.

51. Leah Margulies. "Baby Formula Abroad: Exporting Infant Malnutrition." *Christianity and Crisis* 35 (November 10, 1975).

52. INFACT and ICCR. "Nestlégate." Mimeograph of Internal Memorandum, Nestlé Company, August, 1980.

53. Bruce Vandervort. "US, Almost Alone, Casts Ballot Against Code on Baby Formula. Washington *Post*, 22 May, 1981.

54. Bruce Vandervort. "Final Baby Formula Vote: 118-to-Guess Who?" Washington *Post*, 22 May, 1981.

55. "US Casts 'No' Vote as WHO Approves Baby Formula Code." New York *Times*, 21 May, 1981.

56. "WHO Approves Limits on Sales of Baby Formula." Wall Street *Journal*, 21 May, 1981.

57. "Baby-Formula Code Adopted by WHO With US Casting Only Dissenting Vote." Wall Street *Journal*, 22 May, 1981

58. Bernard D. Nossiter. "UN Dispute Looms on Infant Formula." New York *Times*, 14 May, 1981.

59. Harry Levine, Vice President of Bristol-Myers Company. "Baby Formula: Health Isn't The Issue." Washington *Post*.

60. Stephen C. Joseph, M.D. Statement in opposition to the US Government Position on the WHO/UNICEF International Code on the Marketing of Breast Milk Substitutes. Washington, DC 18 May, 1981, Mimeographed.

61. Eugene N. Babb, Statement at Press Conference of the American Public Health Association. Washington, DC, 18 May, 1981, Mimeographed.

62. "WHO Meeting Backs Infant Formula Code." *CNI Weekly Report* (November/December 1979).

63. Andy Chetley. "Bottling up the formula firms." *UN Development Forum* 8 (June, 1980): 15.

# Chapter V

1. Statement of Anwar Fazal, President, International Organization of Consumers Unions, *in* U.S. House of Representatives, Committee on Foreign Affairs, *Export of Hazardous Products: Hearings Before the Subcommittee on International Economic Policy and Trade*, page 14, 96th Cong. 2nd Sess., June 5, 12, and September 9, 1980.

2. U.S. House of Representatives, Committee on Government Operations, *Report on Export of Products Banned By U.S. Regulatory Agencies*, pages 3, 10, 95th Cong., 2nd Sess., October 4, 1978.

3. *See* Esther Peterson and Robert Harris, Co-Chairs, Interagency Working Group on Hazardous Substances Export Policy, *Background Report On the Executive Order On Federal Policy Regarding the Export of Banned or Significantly Restricted Substances*, pages 12-16, and Appendix A, January 15, 1981.

4. Robert Harris, Member of the Council on Environmental Quality, later became the co-chair of the Interagency Working Group.

5. U.S. House of Representatives, Committee on Government Operations, *supra* note 2.

6. *Id.,* page 3.

7. *See* Federal Pesticide Act of 1978, Pub. L. No. 95-396, 92 Stat. 819 (1978); Consumer Product Safety Authorization Act of 1978, Pub. L. No. 95-631, 92 Stat. 3742 (1978).

8. "U.S. Citizen Arrested In Mexico After Importing Hazardous Wastes", *International Environmental Reporter* April 8, 1981, pages 786, 787; Letter from Lawrence U. Fairhall, Korea Trade Promotion Center to International Activities Office, U.S. Environmental Protection Agency, December 10, 1979.

9. Bill Richards, "U.S. Fights Export of Hazardous Waste," *Washington Post,* January 26, 1980, page 4.

10. H.R. 6587; 126 Cong. Rec. H 1243-4, February 25, 1980. The Barnes bill and the administration's deliberations on a hazardous export policy were the subject of hearings before the House Foreign Affairs Committee, Subcommittee on International Economic Policy and Trade in 1980. *See* footnote 1 *supra.*

11. Joanne Omang, "Carter Limits U.S. Export of Banned Items," *Washington Post,* January 16, 1981, page D1.

12. *Id.*

13. The Interagency Working Group decided to exclude consideration of hazardous industry exports because "the issues they raise and the nature of possible remedial action are quite different than those related to exports of hazardous substances." While noting that limited environmental reviews are already required under Executive Order 12114 for U.S. Government actions in support of the export of certain hazardous production facilities, the Interagency Working Group argued that it otherwise lacked a statutory basis for any such controls and recommended that Congress examine the issue. Peterson and Harris, *supra* note 3, pages 55-56.

   The Interagency Working Group took the same position on infant formula and other products that are not regulated in the United States, but may be dangerous when consumed overseas and stated that: "It appears that commercial trade involving such products might be more appropriately dealt with through such means as technical assistance codes for industry rather than export controls." Peterson and Harris, *supra* note 3, pages 55.

14. Executive Order 12290, February 17, 1981.

15. Prepared Statement of S. Jacob Scherr, Staff Attorney, Natural Resources Defense Council, to the Subcommittee on International Economic Policy and Trade, Committee on Foreign Affairs, U.S. House of Representatives, concerning the Reagan Rescission of the U.S. Hazardous Substances Export Policy, March 12, 1981, page 4.

16. Peter Behr, "Reagan Imposes Strict New Rules on Cabinet, Agency Regulators," *Washington Post,* February 18, 1981, page A1.

17. Petition of the Chemical Manufacturers Association ("CMA") To Amend Regulations Respecting Compliance With Section 12(b) of the Toxic Substances Control Act, 45 *Federal Register* 82844 (December 16, 1980). The CMA petition was submitted to the U.S. Environmental Protection Agency in June 1981. On August 5, 1981, the Natural Resources Defense Council filed a 30-page memorandum with EPA in opposition to the CMA Petition. As of February 1, 1982, the EPA had not taken any action on this matter.

18. *See* Statement of Dr. Jack Early, President, National Agricultural Chemicals Association Before the Subcommittee on Department Operations, Research, and Foreign Agriculture of the Committee on Agriculture, United States House of Representatives, July 16, 1981.

19. Caroline E. Mayer, "Easing of Hazardous Exports Studied," *Washington Post*, September 9, 1981, page Al; R. Jeffrey Smith, "Administration Set To Assist Hazardous Exports," 214 *Science,* October 2, 1981, page 36; "Reagan Opens the Door to a Dangerous Trade," *New Scientist,* September 17, 1981, page 707.

20. H.R. 2439, *see also* Office of Congressman Michael D. Barnes, "House Hearings Set, Barnes To Push Bill On Hazardous Exports," February 20, 1981 (Press Release); Export of Hazardous Wastes Control Act of 1981, S. 622, 127 Cong. Rec. S1836, March 5, 1981.

21. *See* David Kay, *The International Regulation of Pharmaceutical Drugs — A Report to the National Science Foundation on the Application of International Regulatory Techniques to Scientific/Technical Problems,* The American Society of International Law Studies in Transnational Legal Policy No. 14 (Washington, D.C.: West Publishing Company, 1976).

22. *See* Sam Gusman, Konrad Ian Moltke, Francis Irwin, Cynthia Whitehead, *Public Policy for Chemicals: National and International Issues.* (Washington D.C.: The Conservation Foundation, 1980.)

23. *The Standard* (Nairobi, Kenya), May 11, 1977, page 3.

24. UNEP Governing Council Decision No. 85(V), May 25, 1977.

25. UNEP Governing Council Decision No. 6/4, May 24, 1978.

26. U.N. General Assembly Resolution No. 34/173, December 1979.

27. U.N. General Assembly Resolution No. 34/186, December 15, 1980.

28. U.N. General Assembly Resolution No. 36/166, December 16, 1981.

29. Draft Report of the Ad Hoc Meeting of Senior Government Officials Expert in Environmental Law, UNEP/IG 28/L.5, November 6, 1981

30. Comments of Dr. P.L. de Reeder, Chairman of the Business and Industry Advisory Committee to the OECD and G. Dominquez, Chairman of the International Affairs Group, Chemical Manufacturers Association/SOCMA, at the Seminar on Controls of Chemicals in Importing Countries, Dubrovnik, Yugoslavia, April 22-25, 1981.

31. The struggle over WHO's infant formula code is described in Chapter Four.

32. Khor Kok Peng, "Penang Consumer's Association," Centre Report, Vol. 4, No. 4, Nairobi, Kenya, Environmental Liaison Centre, December 1979; Robert Richter, "Pesticides and Pills: For Export Only," (Transcript of documentary films) October 1981; Charles Medawar, "Tracking Technology," *Outlook,* No. 4, Penang, Malaysia, December 1971/January 1980.

33. Robert Richter, "Pesticides and Pills: For Export Only," (Transcript of documentary films), October 1981.

34. Jonathan Ratner and William Taylor, "Bucking the Drug Industry, An Interview with Dr. Zafrullah Chandhury" 1 *Multinational Monitor* No. 7, August 1980.

35. International Organization of Consumer Unions (IOCU), "The New Wave of the International Consumer Movement" (Summary of the President's Closing Remarks at the 10th IOCU World Congress, The Hague, June 22-26, 1981), The Hague, Netherlands: IOCU, June 26, 1981.

36. "New 'International Antibody' Will Resist Ill-Treatment of Consumers by Multinational Drug Companies" (Press Statement Released at Conclusion of Conference in Geneva Sponsored by BUKO), Geneva, Switzerland, May 29, 1981.

# INDEX

161

Velsicol Chemical Corporation, 2,
  15, 32
Venezuela, 39
Verdivitone, 53
Vietnam, 33


Wastes, 69, 72; asbestos, 62, 64,
  65; chemical, 83; from paint in-
  dustry, 72; solid, 62, toxic, 61,
  70, 71, 72, 73, 74, 85
Wellcome Wallace, 53
West Germany, 6, 7, 8, 9, 13, 17,
  27, 41, 43, 44, 52, 71, 74, 93
Wide, Katarina, 51
Winstrol, 41
Wohler, Fredrich, 3
Washington, DC, 72; Sanitary
  Commission, 72
*Washington Post*, 74
Waste-recycling, 71
Waste water discharge, 62, 65
Water pollution, 69
Workplace standards, 65
World Health Assembly, 80
World War I, 4
Word War II, 4, 5, 6, 8, 83